Ad
Six-Figure Solo: T... ...
Surviving to Thriving

Okeoma Moronu Schreiner, Attorney, Podcaster, Speaker: *The Happy Lawyer Project*

[*Six-Figure Solo: Transform Your Practice from Surviving to Thriving*] is an easy read with great actionable tips. I'm not a solo practitioner but I believe the book is filled with thought-provoking strategies for any lawyers struggling with overwhelm, burnout, or under-earning in their legal practice.

Karima Gulick, Registered Patent Attorney, Gulick Law

Ally Lozano has done it again! In her new book, *Six-Figure Solo: Transform Your Practice from Surviving to Thriving*, Ally lays out an actionable, step-by-step plan to take your law practice to the next level. This is the book I wish I had when I first launched my business, but I'm really glad to have it now while I'm optimizing my systems, streamlining my processes, and growing my practice. *Six-Figure Solo* is very well-written, very well-thought out, and more than just theory—the book gives you concrete examples to build a thriving business. *Six-Figure Solo* is full of great practical information. Highly recommended for anyone starting a practice or looking to take their practice to the next level!

Carolyn Elefant, Law Offices of Carolyn Elefant, MyShingle.com

Unlike many other books of the law-business genre, *Six-Figure Solo: Transform Your Practice from Surviving to Thriving* doesn't laud the importance of running a law firm as a business and stop there. Instead, [Ally Lozano] gives lawyers the tools to actually operate their practices like a well-run business machine with detailed checklists, sales scripts, and workflow sheets that can be readily adapted to most practice areas.

SIX FIGURE SOLO

*Transform Your Practice from
Surviving to Thriving*

ALEXANDRA LOZANO, ESQ.

ALLY LOZANO LLC

Published by Ramses House Publishing LLC, Baltimore, MD, www.publishingforlawyers.com

First Printing, 2019

ISBN 978-1-7320825-3-3 paper; 10-digit: 1-7320825-3-7

Notice: The book is written for attorneys who are in business for themselves. Its purpose is to educate attorneys on how to transform their law practices into thriving businesses by implementing the six steps highlighted within.

Library of Congress Preassigned Control Number: 2019904735

Printed and bound in the United States of America

DISCLAIMER: The opinions expressed herein are solely the author's opinions and are based on her personal experience. The information contained in this book is provided for informational purposes only, and should not be construed as legal advice on any matter. The transmission and receipt of information, in whole or in part, via the Internet or through e-mail does not constitute or create a lawyer-client relationship.

The sample documents and materials in Six-Figure Solo are just that—samples. Read each one carefully and adapt it to meet your specific needs. Be sure to check your state's bar rules before using any of the samples herein. The law can change quickly, so always review the relevant rules and regulations.

Ally Lozano LLC
707 S. Grady Way, Ste. 600
Renton, WA 98057

RAMSES HOUSE PUBLISHING LLC
"SELF-PUBLISHING EXPERTS FOR LAWYERS"
WWW.RAMSESHP.COM

For *Lauren Eagan*,
a dear friend,
an excellent lawyer, and
a Six Figure Solo

You cannot get sick enough to help sick people get better. You cannot get poor enough to help poor people thrive. It is only in your thriving that you have anything to offer anyone. If you're wanting to be of an advantage to others, be as tapped in, turned in, turned on as you can possibly be.

—Abraham Hicks

SUMMARY OF CONTENTS

FOREWORD

Carolyn Elefant
Law Offices of Carolyn Elefant
MyShingle.com

Even the most traditional lawyers have finally gotten the message that running a law firm is just like running a business; yet few are actually doing so. Of course, some stubborn lawyers—whether practicing solo or as partners at blue-chip firms—simply refuse to accept the reality that law is a business. So they continue to struggle to survive.

At the same time, many lawyers recognize how important business savvy is to a successful law practice, and they are eager to incorporate sound business principles ... if only they knew how.

That's where attorney Ally Lozano's second book, *Six Figure Solo: Transform Your Practice from Surviving to Thriving*, comes into play. Unlike many other books of the law-business genre, *Six Figure Solo* doesn't laud the importance of running a law firm as a business and stop there. Instead, this book gives lawyers the tools to actually operate their practices like a well-run business machine with detailed checklists, sales scripts, and workflow sheets that can be readily adapted to most practice areas.

Lozano's book also addresses the other barrier that prevents lawyers from running their firms like a business: the billable hour.

Think about it: Does Apple set prices based on the amount of time it takes to produce a Mac or an Apple Watch? Does your local bakery list the hours that the staff spent chopping apples and kneading dough to make a pie? Of course not.

These businesses set prices to cover their costs and generate profit. That's how businesses operate. Yet, many lawyers and business advisors, who purport to teach lawyers how to run their firms as businesses, continue to endorse hourly rates.

But not Lozano. She is a staunch proponent of the flat fee because of the benefits a flat-fee model provides to lawyers (administrative ease and upfront payment) and clients (certainty in price and availability of the lawyer). Although Lozano doesn't attempt to persuade all lawyers to adopt flat fees, she offers detailed steps on how to implement flat fees in many practices.

To be sure, some lawyers may be uncomfortable with Lozano's discussion of "sales," which many lawyers find unseemly. But as Lozano points out, incorporating sales into your consultations is a way to educate clients and build relationships. Again, as with many of the other recommendations, readers can adapt Lozano's sales scripts to their particular practices and personalities.

As a law firm owner who has blogged about solo and small firm practice at MyShingle.com for 16 years, I strongly believe that solos and small firms play a critical role in ensuring that our justice system can be accessed by regular individuals and not just the wealthy or deep-pocketed corporations. But in order for solo and small firm lawyers to serve that role, solo and small firm practice must be sustainable and profitable. This book ensures that result.

ACKNOWLEDGMENTS

My life is infinitely blessed because of my family.

To my husband, Manuel, my greatest inspiration and support: I love you with all my heart. I love doing everything together. You have taken all of my many ideas, refined them, and helped make them better. Thank you for encouraging me every day to be the best version of myself. You are the greatest man I have ever known. Thank you for everything that you do for me.

To my children, Magaly, Noelia, Khloe, Isabella, and Quique: You are beautiful souls. I love teaching you about social justice and the ways that we can help change the world while also teaching you business lessons. I love each of you so deeply.

To my parents, who raised me and gave everything for me: Thank you for supporting me and for always being there for me no matter what. I am the person I am today thanks to you encouraging me to chase down my passions and interests. You taught me joy and deep interest in life, which is one of the greatest gifts you could have given me.

To Amy Rios: You make it all so easy. You are my rock. Thank you for all of your great ideas, for keeping me focused on the positive, and for always being in my corner. You have made me laugh during too many consultations! You are there for the good and the bad, the ups and the downs, and I know I can always count on you. Thank you for everything.

To my AMIGAs: You teach me every day how I can be a better lawyer, create new strategies, think outside the box, and more. You have made me a better person and a better mother. Walking alongside each and every one of you is humbling and one of the great joys of my life. Thank you for showing up with your knowledge, authenticity, and support. You are the best women I know.

To my in-office team: You are incredible, passionate women who show up ready to give 100 percent every single day. I do not know how I could ever be so lucky in life or business to have found you. Though the people who are the luckiest are our clients—you give them incredible customer service and truly care about them. Thank you for everything that you do every day to change the lives of our clients and ensure that our office runs smoothly. The only reason everything that I teach works is because I have all of you working so hard to make sure it does. Thank you for everything that you do.

PREFACE

> "Being a solo practitioner does not have to mean
> going it alone."

If you love law as much as I do, you're no stranger to personal sacrifice. You've put in endless hours working for someone else, missing birthdays and perhaps losing yourself in the process. And if you're already out on your own, you've likely given clients way too much control as you put their needs first. Sound familiar?

I used to be right where you are. Long before becoming a seven-figure law firm owner, I was killing myself working for law firms that were cutthroat, unhappy, and underpaid work environments. I questioned, "Is this what being a lawyer is really all about?" Of course not.

But even without a clear alternative in sight, I decided that no level of job security was worth my personal sense of well-being. I quit and headed out on my own.

While my leap of faith has ultimately carried me far, my first years of running a solo business were a personal training ground of trial and error. Lots and lots of error! I was practicing law from Mexico and expecting my first child when a hurricane took our material possessions (that's *all* it took, thankfully). I no longer had the luxury of "just getting by." I quickly decided that I would run my law firm as a true business and no longer as some sort of legal charity center. And the rest, as they say, is history.

Lawyers by our very nature are leaders. In general, we are Type A, high-achieving individuals who are oftentimes perfectionists. We are trained to win in an adversarial system. Our words are our most lethal weapons. We know how to take a position and argue for it vehemently despite any contrary logic or reason that may be presented to us.

For these precise reasons, lawyers can often struggle as bosses and managers because it is hard for us to admit that we are wrong. We think that if we were to concede one point we would lose the entire argument. This is simply untrue.

Regardless of whether you are an associate, partner, or solo practitioner, our jobs require us to manage people in some way. We have legal assistants, paralegals, secretaries, junior associates, senior attorneys—and many combinations thereof—who look to us to lead and give direction.

This book focuses on accountability

Our jobs require a high level of accountability. "Getting it right" is critically important right down to the smallest detail. If we make even a minor mistake, it could cost us a case. That kind of pressure is intense! It is often easier to shift the blame to someone else instead of focusing on a way that we could actively participate in helping to ensure an error-free work environment.

Let's use an example of a case that was submitted to the court with a few pages of evidence that were upside-down. As the attorney, you likely counted on your paralegal to properly and effectively file the packet. Maybe you reviewed the legal argument portion of the packet and the table of contents but did not check to make sure everything was perfect because you assumed your paralegal had it covered.

At this point, it is easy to blame the paralegal who clearly made the mistake. But if you take responsibility as well, it will help you focus on solutions instead of just problems.

Could the mistake have been caused by a lack of communication of expectations? Maybe your paralegal was under the impression that you would do a final quality review. By discussing your expectations of one another, you become more solutions-oriented instead of merely seeking to lay blame.

This book focuses on growing your business

"You've got to spend money to make money!" That is my husband's rallying cry to me whenever I am hesitating to invest in something for my business. This constant reminder has pushed me out of my comfort zone and into the profit zone.

If you're at a crossroads, trying to decide if you should invest in a tool to make your business better and easier, let go of the fear and take the crucial step to grow your business.

I remember when my firm started growing and things were progressing, yet I was suffering from total financial chaos. I wasn't billing my clients properly or regularly. I was undercharging and I knew it, but I didn't know how to get out of it. I felt ashamed. I thought that if I had been smarter, I would have been better at building a business. I felt embarrassed to ask for help because I didn't want people to know how bad it was. My shame held me hostage; I felt I couldn't reach out to anyone for help.

I knew other lawyers, but we had never talked business. We talked cases. We talked strategy. It almost felt dirty to talk about money, finances, pricing, and more.

This is why I choose to talk openly about money and finances—I wish someone had told me these things.

Through trial and error, I have learned a great deal about running a successful business. I've learned that excuses lead to mediocrity and under-earning. I've learned that no one will hold me accountable the way I do for the things I do or don't do. I've learned that there's no place for pessimism in running a business if you intend to be successful at it. And I've learned to be open-minded and willing to try new things.

More powerful than any new management system, or technique I can teach you, is this underlying truth that you are not simply running a law firm, but a business. Done correctly, it becomes your key to unlocking the door to a truly better life.

Being a solo practitioner does not have to mean going it alone. And I can't wait to help you get started.

CONTENTS

INTRODUCTION

"You did not become an attorney to be poor."

For some reason, so many lawyers are under the assumption that making money is somehow wrong. We think that rich lawyers only get rich by taking advantage of people. We believe that if we want to serve people honorably, we must do so without pay. We must do so even to the point that it harms our profits and our time with our loved ones. We think that we have to make ourselves poor in order to truly care about the work we do.

This is just baloney. It is completely untrue. We can care about our clients, care about the work, and also care about making a profit. We do great work for our clients. Doing great work and earning a great living aren't mutually exclusive propositions. We can do both. In fact, we *must* do both for our own survival and for the sake of our families.

My experience in running a successful business comes from a combination of on-the-job learning, advice from other successful lawyers and professionals, and reading numerous books written by entrepreneurs and applying those principles to the business of law.

Just like all first-time business owners, I searched for advice. I went looking for a secret to success that I believed had to exist somewhere. I thought that if someone could just tell me the steps to how to build a successful law firm, I would do it.

Unfortunately, I never found that resource anywhere, so I worked hard to uncover the secrets for myself.

The reason I share my experiences as a business owner is because I have had to discover so much on my own of what works and what doesn't.

When I began this journey, I had no idea what I was doing. I wasn't keeping up with my bookkeeping. I didn't understand the concept of a profit margin or its importance. I didn't pay myself a salary. I didn't track anything in my law firm.

I think running a business is even more difficult when you don't know what it is that you don't know but should know. Every time I have experienced success in my business, I have felt that there was another level right above me, one that I couldn't see. It always seemed to be hovering just above my head, a dark ceiling that I needed to reach but didn't have enough information to realize it even existed.

Learning how to understand, track, and follow the numbers in my business has allowed me to break through that dark ceiling and shed light on what makes my business thrive.

In my first book, *Be the CEO: Gain Control, Turn a Profit, and Reclaim Your Life*, I focused on how to think and act like a CEO and the different roles a lawyer takes on in order to build a successful business.

In this, my second book, *Six-Figure Solo: Transform Your Practice from Surviving to Thriving*, I take what it means to be the CEO of Your Law Firm to a higher level with a focus on what it means to truly be in control of your law firm, your finances, and your life.

"*Step 1: Getting Paid*" offers revolutionary ways to ensure that you are paid what you are worth. It explores the flat-fee model, different client payment options, ways to stay top of mind with current and past clients, ways to perform pro bono purposefully, how to follow up on leads, and it covers the advantages of paying yourself a salary.

"Step 2: Taking Your Law Firm's Brand to the Next Level" takes a hard look at your brand to figure out whether your messaging is working (*i.e.*, low cost/high volume vs. high end/low volume) and whether the model you've chosen is by choice or by necessity. It covers how to use your writing and advocacy skills to position yourself as an expert to gain media coverage. It explains the importance of building a following on social media and offers ways of building an email list. Last but not least, Step 2 provides guidance on protecting your brand and responding to bad reviews.

"Step 3: Conquering Sales with Confidence and Authenticity" shows you how to incorporate sales and value-based price quoting into your consultations; how to overcome objections; and how to use creative upselling to offer current clients additional, yet relevant, services.

"Step 4: It's All About the Client" takes a deep dive into the problems that plague lawyer/client communication and how to recognize, fix, and avoid those problems. It places emphasis on the speed at which a lawyer should contact a client with bad news or after a misunderstanding. And it focuses on the importance of customer service and ongoing nurturing of the lawyer/client relationship.

"Step 5: Streamlining Your Law Firm" gets into the nitty-gritty of hiring and firing, assessing your firm's needs to avoid over-hiring, maximizing your current employees, choosing the right clients, and minimizing your dependence on paper.

"Step 6: Achieving Success in Work and Life: Accepting Accountability & Responsibility" jumps head first into spotting reasons why your firm might not be performing as well as it should be and why you may be under-earning; how you can decrease the deficiencies and increase the efficiencies in your law firm to maximize your time and your profits; and how to systematize your law firm and gain more time to perform the activities that are important to you.

Because you are reading this book, you've reached a point in your law practice where you're done with battling with your bottom line.

You want to love more than just your work; you want to love your life. You did not become an attorney to be poor.

The more you know about what it takes to run a successful business, the better off you'll be and the more satisfied you'll be with your law practice. Business-minded attorneys do more than just practice law. They create and sustain financially successful businesses.

This book is titled *Six-Figure Solo: Transform Your Practice from Surviving to Thriving* because the advice and actionable steps you find in these pages will ensure your sustainability. Becoming a Six-Figure Solo is an attainable goal, one that can be reached through hard work, dedication, and the ability to let go of the things that are holding you back from reaching your level of success.

Each of us might be at different points in our practices, yet this book provides actionable advice for attorneys of all levels and in different fields of practice. At the heart of the book is the goal to make you a better business owner; to show you that you are not simply running a law practice, you are building a sustainable business.

STEP 1

GETTING PAID

"Obsessing over pricing is obsessing over the wrong thing."

Attorneys always think about price as if it is the only thing that drives a client's decision to hire them. This may come as a surprise, but clients actually want *much more* than low prices. They want support and attention.

Clients aren't necessarily looking for the cheapest route. In fact, clients would rather pay more for impeccable customer service and peace of mind. They would rather pay more to have their calls returned quickly. They would rather pay more to have the attorney work after hours on an urgent matter. They would rather pay more to know that the attorney has the situation under control and they can stop worrying about it.

For example, a colleague and I were discussing her firm's pay structure and I suggested that she increase her fees on a particular case she was handling. "I think the client will be surprised because she doesn't see me that way," my colleague said, meaning that she's not viewed as an attorney who would charge extra fees or one who would charge higher fees. "She sees me as laid-back and she will be shocked by the price."

I told my colleague, "The client doesn't really think of you that way; the client doesn't really think of you at all. The client sees you as a solution to a problem, a solution that comes with a price."

"Do you see?" I asked. "We are thinking about pricing one way while clients are thinking about pricing an entirely different way, in that we feel we can't charge them for our work."

When you obsess over pricing, you are obsessing over the wrong thing. People are willing to pay to have their problems solved. Think about the times you've worked with a lawyer. Yes, price matters—but if the price will get you the solution you seek, the price is acceptable.

When we focus on money only, we are narrowly focusing on one possible problem that the client has—either a lack of money or simply not wanting to part with their money.

We are failing to take into account the other problems that the client has that we can and should solve—in particular, the legal problem.

Most solos—women solos, in particular—cut fees because they feel bad for their clients. They feel bad about charging more. They believe they are doing a better service to the client by charging low fees.

When you have low fees, you must balance that with high volume in order to survive—and when you have very high volume, the first thing sacrificed is customer service. The second thing is your sanity.

"Step 1: Getting Paid" discusses ways of increasing your firm's business by setting the right fees for your services; implementing a flat-fee structure for your firm; ensuring that your fees are paid; utilizing existing networks for referrals; being more intentional in your pro bono work; and carving out a salary for yourself.

We will cover:

1. Exploring the Flat-Fee Model;
2. Revolutionizing Your Practice by Getting Paid in Full;
3. Getting More Clients by Cultivating Existing Clients;

4. Using Pro Bono or Low Bono in Your Practice Purposefully;
5. Following Up on Leads; and
6. Determining Your Profit Margin and Paying Yourself.

Exploring the Flat-Fee Model

There are great arguments for hourly billing, and there is no "right answer" to whether it is better to bill flat or hourly. Ultimately, only you know what works best for you and your practice. However, I feel very strongly that the traditional hourly billing model is outdated, archaic, and inefficient. But in order to work with a flat-fee model and ensure that it works for you and your firm, you have to make sure you set the right fee.

Those of us who work on flat fees often struggle to find the right price point. Most of us are drastically undercharging and undervaluing our services. But if you want to give flat fees a try, it is imperative to set the right fee; otherwise, you will end up with a high-volume, low-value practice.

Below are a few tips to help make flat fees work for you:

1. Consider ALL work that must be done in the case

We often estimate the time that it will take to complete the legal work on the case, including preparing applications and forms, gathering and preparing evidence, writing briefs and legal arguments, and more.

But the number-one mistake that I see attorneys make with flat-fee billing is they don't fully account for all the administrative tasks associated with the case.

Usually, our flat-fee price fails to account for the client communications that are a huge part of the case. That includes clients who want to call to check in every week; clients who show up without notice; clients who don't give you the evidence and you have to hound them for it.

Even when the client is an easy client, there is still a lot of communication that goes on outside of case preparation. Also, sending monthly update letters is an important task that takes time (printing, signing, preparing the envelope, mailing, etc.). Your fees should be adjusted accordingly.

Some cases will take years to resolve and you will need to be communicating with those clients regularly about their case status; this means over the course of years, your clients will be calling to check in, will want to have meetings, etc. All of this must be contemplated—and included—in your flat fee. It is the human factor of legal work that you must account for.

Once a person has hired you, he or she sees you as the lawyer for all things, and any law-related question will make him or her give you a call. Set a fee that includes random calls, customer service, and a thoughtful customer experience.

Want to send me an email a day? Sure thing! No problem. I've got it covered. Want to bombard me with random questions? I welcome it. This is because I expect this behavior from clients. You should, too. If you price accordingly, you will turn a "high-maintenance" client into a manageable one.

I know you care about your clients. So give them that support. Give them the help they need—the calls, the emails, and the reassurance. And set a fee that takes all of that into consideration.

*admin fee - fedex etc.

2. Not all flat fees are equal

It is easy to fall into the trap of setting one flat fee for a case type and then not budging from that price. This approach fails to consider the facts and circumstances of the particular case that is in front of you. Some factors that should cause your flat fee to increase are:

- Urgent cases that require work on nights, weekends, and holidays.

- High-maintenance clients: Lawyers always complain about "high-maintenance" clients. But if you charge a high-maintenance client the right fee, it's not a problem.

- Length of case: Some cases, by their very nature, cannot be resolved quickly. For immigration attorneys, we are seeing a very long wait for U visas, for example. Because of the additional work and client contact required in a long case, your fee should be higher.

- Likelihood of additional work: Depending on your practice area, there may be additional work that could come up later in the case but that is not required at the outset. This could be something that can be anticipated from the beginning, something that happens in many cases, though not every case. There are certain case types that often receive requests for additional evidence or discovery, additional hearing dates, etc. If you do not want to charge for that work separately, you need to estimate the amount of time and resources required to complete that extra work in the event it occurs. Otherwise, you should make it clear in your client agreement what work is NOT covered and what might require an additional fee.

3. Increase your prices

Review all your pricing and see where you can increase the price to more accurately reflect the time it takes to work on that case type. It often is difficult for us to raise our fees because we are afraid clients won't pay it or that they can't afford it. Start slow and add even $100 at a time. Schedule a time in two months to review your pricing again.

4. Stay strong in your pricing

The most common misstep in flat-fee pricing is not charging enough. I know this from personal experience and also from working with attorneys on an individual basis. The flat fee often falls short because we negotiate it down even before we present it to the client, thereby lowering our set prices in the moment.

Usually, we lower the price without even giving the client a chance to object to it or ask for a discount or cheaper price. I call this "negotiating against ourselves." In our heads, we start to tell ourselves all the reasons why a client can't or won't pay, and then we cut the price.

Many of us struggle with sticking to our pre-determined prices. This is especially true for us women. We begin to take into account the client's personal circumstances, our personal feelings about the case, the injustice of the system, etc., and then we slash our prices.

It is important to hold hard to your prices and say them with confidence. This mostly boils down to valuing your work. You provide an important, life-changing service. You deserve to be paid for it.

5. Create a price list

A price list is a tool that will help hold you accountable to your pricing. This is for your internal use only, not for the clients; however, it is a point of reference for you to use when you go into a consultation or quote a price. It keeps you from negotiating against yourself.

Remember: The work that you do is important. You are exchanging value for value. Your clients are investing in life-changing services, and you are providing them with excellent work product.

Lesson Learned: You don't get more money if you don't ask for more money

I was invited by two attorneys to visit their law firms and help them restructure their businesses. Both attorneys are well-known in their communities for their work, yet both were severely, yes, severely, undercharging.

There were two cases in one firm that needed a change in strategy. The attorney had charged each client $3,500 and each had paid $500 on their cases. She was feeling bad to even ask for the next payment of $500. She was going on and on about how she felt the clients couldn't afford it.

I told this attorney what I would charge for each of her cases using the new strategy—$8,500 paid in full or $9,500 on a payment plan. The attorney didn't want to charge her clients that because she truly believed they wouldn't pay it. She agreed, however, that my price more correctly reflected the work that needed to be done in each of the cases.

I asked her to let me "pitch"[1] the new fees to her clients. She agreed, and I took the two appointments back to back, quoted the new prices, and they both paid them. Right there. In full.

The attorney was stunned.

The next attorney had a very complex and urgent case, added to that an extremely high-maintenance client. She knew she needed a high fee but the client already owed her money from a previous matter and was complaining about paying the money she still owed. I said, "Listen, let's be real. In order to do the work that needs to be done within the timeframe and with this client, the amount you need is $7,500. Let me talk to her. I want you to get paid what you deserve."

During the phone call, I quoted the fee to the client and she immediately began to complain that she didn't have the money. I could tell that the attorney was nervous and wanted us to cave and give a payment plan or cut the fee. But she let me continue.

I told the client we needed the payment in two hours in order to complete the case in the urgent timeframe we had. The client said, "Okay, I'm going to make

---

[1] Learn more about how to develop your pitch in Chapter 3, "Conquering Sales with Confidence and Authenticity."

some calls and I will get back to you." Within two hours, the client called and gave the entire payment.

The attorney was shocked.

And guess what? The client started calling the next morning at 6:00 am to check in on her case, just as the attorney anticipated, and the attorney didn't mind taking the call. She wasn't frustrated, overwhelmed, or feeling like the client was "too much." She had finally priced her fees in a way that made the work worth it.

These attorneys were stuck in under-earning because they didn't see any other way. They didn't think that a client would pay a higher fee.

The truth is that you MUST ask for the fee. You are in charge of what you are worth.

Revolutionizing Your Practice by Getting Paid in Full

I want you to get rid of your payment plans.

Does this sound crazy? Believe me, I thought so, too. But bear with me for a moment while I explain.

For some reason, we, as lawyers, are stuck in this backwards way of thinking that payment plans are a requirement. In my career, I was taught to give a price and then offer a payment plan. And the payment plan was always at least half down and then a reasonable payment per month, maybe $350 on the low side to around $500 or higher. That was the wisdom that was imparted to me.

Some lawyers have been told by their mentors that "if someone wants to hire you and only has $100, you take the $100!"

This means that for many lawyers, even asking their clients for a down payment of half the contract amount is very difficult for them.

1. Ask for full payment up front

Can you imagine asking your clients to pay in full up front? It sounds far-fetched, but that is exactly what I began doing and couldn't believe the positive response from many of my clients. It really works!

No more messing around with payment plans, no more struggling to make ends meet. If you do a payment plan for the course of a year, you will likely have completed the work and still not be fully paid for it.

When my business manager suggested switching to an upfront payment model, I thought he was crazy. I said, "No one would ever pay in full. That is so far outside the realm of possibility that it will never happen."

I would have bet money on it. And I would have lost.

I was open to testing the idea, so we worked together on a two-price model—one price for when the client pays in full and a higher price for the client to take advantage of a payment plan. We worked up the quote sheets, I practiced my pitch, and I started implementing it in my firm. Immediately, we began to see results. People were paying in full. Over and over and over.

I could not believe it. When I tell lawyers that my clients pay in full, sometimes $15,000 or $20,000, they are completely shocked. One lawyer, who asked me to consult with her on her pricing, needed $7,500 for an urgent matter but was only willing to ask the client for $2,500. She thought that was all the client could pay. So I pitched the client for her asking for payment in full using the two-price model. The client paid the $7,500 in full right then.

The lawyer said to me, "I've never made so much money in one transaction!" I responded, "You have never asked for it before."

On your quote sheets, have your payment-in-full price and have your payment-plan price. Have it very clear right there for clients to see. Be prepared to clearly describe the benefits of paying in full.

I have six-figure months every single month. One reason is because we receive large cash infusions from people paying in full. When I say cash, I don't necessarily mean actual cash—I mean payments, whether by credit card or check.

A system like this begs the question, "What if I have to return the unearned fee?" This is the wrong question. What you should ask is, "How can I earn the fee as quickly as possible?"

If you skip ahead to "Step 5: Streamlining Your Law Firm," you will find advice and tips on how to set up your law firm to earn more than 90 percent of your fee in the first month. Step 5 discusses implementing systems to run your law business more efficiently. With a little bit of structure and planning, you can earn your fee fast.

So forget about returning the fee—instead focus on getting paid in full and earning that fee as quickly as possible.

2. Provide access to legal financing

For those clients who cannot use a credit card or write a check on the spot, there's still an option for payment in full. There are several companies that offer legal financing. The American Bar Association (ABA) recently issued a formal opinion declaring legal financing ethically compliant.[2]

After learning about this, I partnered with a company called *iQualify Lending.* iQualify Lending is a company that offers loans to people who need legal services. When I first heard about this, I

---

[2] "Does your client need fee financing? New ABA ethics opinion provides guidance," *ABA Journal* Online, Nov. 27, 2018, *http://bit.ly/ABAnews. See also* ABA Formal Opinion 484, *http://bit.ly/ABAOp484*:

> Lawyers may refer clients to fee financing companies or brokers in which the lawyers have no ownership or other financial interests provided they comply with Model Rules 1.2(c), 1.4(b), 1.5(a) and (b), 1.6, 1.7(a)(2), and 1.9(a). If a lawyer were to acquire an ownership or other financial interest in a finance company or brokerage and thereafter refer clients to that entity to finance the lawyer's fees, the lawyer would be entering into a business transaction with a client, or obtaining a security or pecuniary interest adverse to the client, or both. In that instance, the lawyer would also be required to comply with Model Rule 1.8(a).

wanted to learn more because I knew that this would revolutionize the practice of law. iQualify helps your clients apply for a loan to cover your legal fees.

With a valid Social Security number and proof of income, the client can get approved. It's a transformational way to do business. The loan is paid to the client and then the client pays you in full.

When I started my partnership with iQualify, I explained to the representative that the setup fee of $2,000 would likely turn away many solos. The fee was $2,000 to start and $199 per month with a 4.99 percent transaction charge.

Upon accepting my advice, iQualify now offers two options if you sign up through me:

- A $500 discount on the setup fee with no long-term contract.

OR

- Payment of the setup fee over time with $500 down and $299 per month for the first year, which offers about a $300 discount.[3]

Before you decide to partner with iQualify or a similar company, visit the website and read the small print and any Frequently Asked Questions to ensure that you are not only familiar with the company's terms and conditions but that you are comfortable with the service. You can also call and speak to a representative to find out whether the service is a good fit for your practice.

Whether you use iQualify or simply begin offering your clients the option to pay in full, this will change everything for you. It will allow you to get back to doing the work you love.

---

[3] Sign up using this link to take advantage of the options listed above: *https://www.iqualifylending.com/allylozano/*.

Getting More Clients by Cultivating Existing Clients

Almost any attorney (or business person) can tell you that the number-one way to bring in business is through referrals. However, most businesses spend their marketing efforts and dollars on trying to bring in new clients.

Why not spend your marketing dollars cultivating the clients you already have? In a fundraising training that I attended when I was on the board of directors for a local nonprofit, I learned that a donor should have a "touch" from the organization at a minimum once per month.

The "touch" should be personalized and make the donor feel special, important, and remembered. This advice can be applied to our clients as well. This idea is not an original one—there is a marketing theory about this called *"Engagement Marketing."*

Your current and past clients are your most important asset. In addition to the money that you receive from your clients, clients are your biggest cheerleaders; they are the people who are out in the community spreading your message.

Ironically, the biggest complaint from clients is that their attorneys do not communicate with them enough. Thus, having a monthly "touch" is critical to making sure your clients feel valued and remembered.

Below are a few ideas on how you can make a connection with your clients on a regular basis:

1. Show appreciation

Many business owners send holiday cards, but we also send our clients a postcard with the change of each season. Vistaprint offers postcards starting from $5 for a set of 50. Great care should be taken to ensure that your mailers reinforce your brand, so add your logo to any postcards you have printed.

Spoil your clients with a handwritten note—it is beautiful and unexpected. Though an email is easy and appreciated, something that you write and sign by hand shows that you have taken an extra step to show that you care. But remember to write legibly.

A small gift or other recognition at the end of the case is also something that will make you stand out and close out your client relationship on a positive note (in addition to winning the case!).

2. Acknowledge referrals

If a current client has referred a new client to you, call the current client to thank him or her. Let the client know how much you appreciate his or her trust in your firm. Alternatively, you can send a short thank-you note (a small gift, like a Starbucks gift card, goes a long way).[4]

3. Mark milestones with a personal gift or recognition

Always be aware of what is happening in your clients' lives. Send appropriate gifts to celebrate their milestones, such as a new baby, a wedding, a child's wedding, and the like. For example, we send birthday cards to every client, client's spouse, and client's children.

When a client of mine suffered an injury at work, we sent him a care package with cookies and other goodies. The cost was minimal, about $15, but the package made an invaluable impact on the client.

If you take the time to cultivate the client experience, it will increase client satisfaction with you and your firm and, ultimately, increase referrals.

---

[4] Be sure to comply with your state's bar rules regarding the treatment of referrals.

Using Pro Bono or Low Bono
in Your Practice Purposefully

We all know that pro bono, low bono, and general volunteer opportunities are important. Some would say they are essential and our duty as lawyers.

However, many of us are engaging in low bono and pro bono activities unintentionally because we are charging too little, doing free work without having a pro bono agreement from the beginning, and doing volunteer work until we are stretched too thin.

We are operating as nonprofits and pro-bono attorneys accidentally.

It is fair to say that most lawyers are overachievers; that makes it difficult for us to say "no." We tell ourselves that we *should* be able to handle one more volunteer event. We reason with ourselves that our client *deserves* to get the work done for free as a defense to our failure to charge the client. We cut our fees because we feel bad for the client or that we think the client cannot afford the fee. We choose to *not* bill fully for our time.

You must hold yourself accountable for your pro bono, low bono, and volunteer work and be present and intentional about it. Choose that work without letting it choose you.

Below are a few ways to empower your practice and choose the pro bono cases that you desire:

1. Determine the number and type of pro bono cases you will take each year

By setting a number and case type, it will help you be very purposeful when you are selecting a case. If you choose three for the year, you likely won't take on three within a month. This also helps you set fees appropriately throughout the year because you know that your financial and time constraints will not be challenged by undercutting your prices on other cases during the year.

2. Create a pro bono and low bono accountability system

Create an internal system before offering a low bono price or pro bono service. For example, designate a person from whom you'll need to gain approval each time you want to cut your fee to offer low bono or pro bono services. This person should be someone who is a straight shooter, someone who can think neutrally about the situation. You can discuss your reasons for wanting to do the pro bono or low bono case, and that person will either approve or reject the proposal.

Another idea is to create a checklist or some sort of criteria to help determine whether to charge less or not charge at all. All cases would have to be run through that checklist and maybe even have someone else provide final approval. If you cut your fees too easily or too often, or you fail to charge for your services, a system of accountability will change things for you dramatically.

3. Measure your volunteer work to ensure that it works for you

Volunteer work makes us feel good, but if it is related to building your business, your brand, and your name recognition, it needs to be tracked to see if it is resulting in new business.

You can do this by maintaining a record of how someone found out about you. Add the question to your intake sheet and then track the responses using a spreadsheet in Microsoft Excel or Google Sheets. If you have some of the more sophisticated products, such as Lawmatics, Clio, or Practice Panther, these can help you maintain a record of client responses as well.

Remember to check your records every few months to see if that specific volunteer work is turning into results for your firm.

Lesson Learned: Stop beating a dead horse

I once volunteered to teach a citizenship class at my local library. I helped people prepare for the citizenship test. The classes were held weekly and I had to commute to a local suburb to teach, which took about 30 minutes. I love teaching, so at first I thoroughly enjoyed the experience. However, with time, it became more tedious and was taking away from expanding my practice, my personal activities that I enjoyed, and time with my family and friends.

When I reached the year point, a friend of mine who was teaching the same class at a different library told me that she was not continuing because it was not making any money for her firm. At first, I was stunned by this. I said, "But don't you care? It will be hard to find another teacher, let alone an immigration attorney teacher at that!" And she said, "I have given it my all for a year. I have not received one client or one referral. I could be doing something else I enjoy that leads to my professional development."

The thought was completely new to me. I realized that I also had not received one case from teaching the course. I actually never even gained one consultation from it. I decided that it was best that I move on to the next opportunity.

4. Develop additional streams of referral sources

When we are first hanging out our shingles, volunteer work, pro bono, and low bono cases can be the main ways that we obtain business. However, with time, it is important to develop other streams of referrals so that you can balance your pro bono time with in-office work on cases that support your business.

Here are a few ideas:

- Connect with attorneys in other practice areas who can be your "go-tos" for other case types, and you can be their "go-to" as well.

- Join bar associations that are outside of your area of practice so you can network with other attorneys.

- Team up with other types of professionals who serve the same population you serve. For example, if you help people who have been injured in an auto accident, link up with chiropractors, massage therapists, and physical therapists in your area who have a dedicated practice of auto accident patients.

5. Offer a free legal clinic

One way to perform pro bono in a deliberate way while also attracting clientele to your firm is to host a free legal clinic.

Though it may seem counterintuitive, hosting a free legal clinic is a way to boost business. You may already participate in community-organized legal clinics as a way to give back to the community and contribute your legal services to those in need, which is a wonderful and altruistic act. However, from a business perspective, volunteering in legal clinics does not usually translate to a steady stream of new business.

By hosting your own free legal clinic, you will attract people who are interested in you and your services. You will build goodwill for your business because the event will be branded by your law firm. Additionally, it has the dual benefit of serving people in need while simultaneously increasing your business.

Below are some tips on how to successfully organize a free legal clinic:

a. Know your audience's availability

Who do you want to attract to your legal clinic? This is an important question to ask because the day of the week and time of day are critical to making your legal clinic a success and should be based on your ideal client's[5] schedule.

---

[5] My book, *Be the CEO of Your Law Firm: Gain Control, Turn a Profit, and Reclaim Your Life*, is the culmination of all my efforts toward building a profitable and sustainable law practice. Chapter 1, "Creating Your Vision and Strategy," offers practical

For our firm, we have found Sunday, 6:00 pm–8:00 pm, to be the best time for a legal clinic.

b. Find an easily accessible place to host the clinic

If your office has ample parking and a large waiting area and conference room, that might be the right place. However, if your elevators only have key-card access on the weekends or the setup isn't right for allowing multiple people to wait at the same time, you may have to seek another location.

The local library can be a great location because it is centrally located and allows you to reserve conference rooms for free. Churches or other places of worship are another great option, although they sometimes impose certain requirements and/or limitations that may not be the right fit. It is ideal to avoid having to pay for a space if possible.

c. Promote the clinic widely

Use your firm's social media pages and email contacts to spread the word about your clinic. My firm's Facebook page is used almost exclusively to promote my free legal events.

You also can contact local radio stations that target your ideal client to ask if they could mention the free legal clinic and/or invite you on to discuss it.

Passing out fliers and putting up posters in local establishments where your ideal clients frequent are other ways to let people know of the clinic (with permission, of course).

You will have to experiment with the amount of time you need to promote the clinic in order to have a good turnout. Because my Facebook page is quite active, I promoted an event with two weeks' notice and had a great turnout.

---

tips and exercises to help you define your Ideal Client and build your ideal law firm. Find *Be the CEO* on Amazon at *https://www.amazon.com/dp/1732082502.*

If you have a large following on social media or a large mailing list, two weeks of promotion can be enough. However, you may need additional time for promotion.

d. Have a system for the day of the event

Be prepared to perform quick consultations at a high volume. Below is a system you can use. It involves the attorney plus two other people; in our case, we had a legal assistant and the business manager.

Example:

Step 1 - The legal assistant is seated at a registration table and greets people as they come in. She provides them with a very detailed intake sheet that asks the majority of the screening questions. It is important to ask these detailed questions on the intake sheet because if you have a good turnout, you will not get to spend more than a few minutes with each person.

Step 2 - When each person returns the intake sheet, the assistant numbers the sheet to designate the person's spot in line.

Step 3 - When each person's number is called, the legal assistant walks the person back to the attorney.

Step 4 - The attorney reviews the intake sheet and asks pointed questions. When she determines eligibility, she very briefly describes an overview of the relief for which the person is eligible, and then walks the person over to the business manager. The attorney takes notes on the intake sheet and notes what the person is eligible for. (Alternatively, if the person is not eligible for anything, the attorney briefly explains his or her rights and provides the person with a business card and some other marketing item, such as a refrigerator magnet or brochure.)

Step 5 - The attorney tells the business manager what the person qualifies for. The business manager then explains to the person the pricing and provides a quote sheet along with a list of all the required documents to get started. The manager presents the quote sheet in a folder that has his business card, the lawyer's business card, a marketing item (like the magnet), and the folder displays the firm's name and address on the front. If the person would like to get started on the case, the person schedules a time to come in. Otherwise, the person leaves fully informed and armed with what he or she needs to begin a case in the future.

Then, the following business day:

Step 6 - The legal assistant prepares a thank-you postcard that she mails to every person who attended the event.

Step 7 - Within a week, either the business manager, attorney, or legal assistant calls each person who was eligible for legal assistance to ask if there are any additional questions and/or schedules an appointment for the person to sign up with the firm.

As you can see, this is a very simple yet effective system that gives all attendees a personalized experience. It is well-branded throughout because everyone receives your business card, a branded folder, and branded information about their legal options, so it helps raise awareness of you and your law firm. It is a win-win for all involved.

Following Up on Leads

The word "lead" may sound too salesy or maybe even seem irrelevant to your law firm, but it is very pertinent to your practice.

1.   What is a lead?

A lead is every single person who is seeking your legal services. In the context of a law firm, whether a solo practice or a larger firm, a lead will consist of someone who contacts your firm by phone, email, or social media to ask about legal services.

In other words, every single phone call that you receive to your law firm is a lead. Every email that you receive asking for information is a lead. Every message that you receive on your firm's Facebook or other social media page is a lead.

If someone contacts your law firm to ask a question, inquire about prices, or find out how to schedule a consultation, that person is a lead.

2. Why do leads matter and why should you follow up?

If someone contacts your law firm, it means that he or she is looking for a lawyer. Yes, it sounds simple enough, but let that sink in. Whether that person is looking for free information or looking to hire right away, what he or she wants is legal advice from a lawyer.

Every single person who contacts your law firm has a high interest in hiring you, or, at the very least, a high interest in paying to talk to you for a consultation.

This means that every phone call, every social media message, and every email could turn into a paid consultation, which then could turn into a paying client. A paid consultation earns money for your law firm. A paying client is what pays your bills.

The word "lead" baffled me the first time I heard it because I had no idea what it meant and no idea what it could mean for my law firm. I gave this idea of leads little to no thought or much importance. Failing to take leads seriously resulted in losing tens of thousands of dollars for my law firm.

Why did we lose thousands of dollars? *Because we did not follow-up on leads!*

Here's where my firm went horribly wrong: If we saw that we had a missed call by someone who did not leave a message with our law firm, *we did not call the person back.*

Our reasoning was, "If they want to talk to us, they will leave a message." We were "too busy" to follow-up with people who weren't interested enough to even leave a message. Maybe you've said the same thing.

So what does it mean to follow-up on leads? Following up on leads means:

- Returning every single missed call

  – Yes, even if there is no message

  – Yes, even if the call came in on a weekend

  – Yes, even if the person calls three times and never leaves a message and you think that it's really annoying

- Returning every text message

- Responding to every email

- Responding to every social media message

3. How can you make this work for you?

If you are a solo, I understand how tedious this sounds. If you have no staff, it feels impossible. However, doing this very small thing will lead to *incredible* results for your bottom line.

To follow-up on leads, it requires someone who is fully dedicated to doing so. If you won't do it, can't do it, or don't want to do it, hire someone who will. Delegate it to someone in your firm. If you have only one staff member, make it part of his or her job and tie bonuses to it. Hire someone, even part-time, to handle the phones. Call every person back.

The point is that every single contact *must* be followed-up on. Every single call *must* be returned. Every single email *must* be responded to. This is *the* way to increase how much money you make in your firm.

Lesson Learned: How we got this right

We had several staff members take turns answering the phone. Our senior paralegal is trained in customer service and is excellent at it, but she had other obligations that only she could do. However, with many staff changes, we ended up passing the phones off to her, and while she did a great job answering the phones, she did not call anyone back who didn't leave a message. And her response time to voicemails was slow. It wasn't the right fit for her.

Then, I hired a business manager. He streamlined the phones in a major way. Then he took it upon himself to return every call that came into the office. Every call is returned within 10 minutes or less, with the average being 3 minutes.

The results? Our consultations increased. Our contracts increased. Our current clients are incredibly happy because every call is returned almost instantly. For a solo practitioner, this sounds overwhelming. However, keep an open mind. Give this a try for just 30 days. You will see positive results.

Determining Your Profit Margin and Paying Yourself

How do you know if your business is profitable? One indicator would be your profit margin. This measure of profitability is typically expressed as a percentage of your revenue. In other words, it's the percentage of revenue earned after all business expenses, *e.g.*, costs, salaries, taxes, depreciation, interest, and other expenses, have been deducted.

The basic calculation is this:

Profit Margin = (Total Revenue – Total Expenses)/Total Revenue

For example, if your Profit and Loss statement (or P&L) shows revenue of $600,000, and your expenses for the year are $375,000, your gross profit would be $225,000. To calculate your profit margin, divide the $225,000 by your total revenue of $600,000, which gives you a profit margin of 0.375 or 37.5 percent.

Many business gurus recommend subtracting anything that can be considered a business expense. But I suggest you focus on your "true" profit margin, which is when you subtract only "necessary" expenses from your total revenue.

I say "necessary" expenses because business owners tend to write off things that are *arguably* a business expense. For example, if you go to dinner where you talk work and pleasure, you can expense it, but you know you probably spent the majority of the time talking about non-work things.

Expensing a conference held at a tropical location, or in a foreign country, is not a "necessary" expense because you can get your continuing legal education credits sitting in front of your computer screen or somewhere locally.

"Necessary" expenses means payroll, which is always the biggest expense, rent or mortgage, electricity, internet service, professional memberships, and anything else that is required to make your firm run.

Looking at your P&L is just the starting point, but look at it realistically to see what things are truly required to make your business run. That's where you will find your "true" profit margin.

1. What if you don't have a P&L statement?

As a business owner, you should have a P&L statement. One of the best ways to handle your daily accounting is to use a reasonably priced service such as *Bench*.[6] If you are trying to do your own bookkeeping, stop right now and get *Bench*. If you aren't doing bookkeeping at all, start right now with *Bench*.

But if you don't have a P&L statement, this exercise is still simple. Calculate your profit margin by looking at your bank account statements for all your deposits, withdrawals, and check payments. Remember to check your business credit card statements as well.

---

[6] Get 20 percent off bookkeeping services from *Bench* for six months after a 30-day trial. Mention Amiga or Ally Lozano.

2. Should you pay yourself a salary?

Paying yourself is one of the most important things you will do as a business owner. You *must* pay yourself. It doesn't matter what your business structure is—S corp., C corp., or partnership—you must pay yourself a salary.

From a business perspective, your goal should be a *fair market value* salary. Determine what it would cost to replace you in case something catastrophic happened, and then pay yourself that amount.

Many of us are not paying ourselves at all. We are settling for what is leftover at the end of each month instead of being more strategic. I understand this because I did the same thing. I was really scared to pay myself a salary because (1) I felt I couldn't afford to and (2) I felt the payroll taxes would break me.

But when it comes to running a business, you are always going to find the money for things your business needs—so start treating yourself as a business need and spend some of that hard-earned money on you.

If the fair market value determination is too much for you right now, start with something more reasonable. Some lawyers I know pay themselves only about $500 every two weeks. That is unreasonable because they can't live on that amount. It's only $13,000 a year!

Lesson Learned: Let the pros handle it

Reaching the point to where I began paying myself a salary was very difficult. I started with a payroll service through Bank of America, which still expected me to report my own payroll taxes, file certain forms, and handle all sorts of responsibilities that were super overwhelming for me. I had no idea what I was doing; I needed something simpler. That's when I found *Gusto*[7] and I have never been happier! *Gusto* makes the payroll process so much easier and the service is very affordable. Whether you have just your own salary or several employees to pay, *Gusto* will provide impeccable service.

---

[7] Get a $100 gift card to Amazon for signing up for payroll, benefits, and HR services.

3. What about taking owner draws or dividends?

As your firm's revenue increases, you might be tempted to keep your salary low and take high draws (or dividends depending on how your business is structured). This strategy is often recommended because your salary tends to be taxed higher than your ownership draws. However, low salaries and high owner draws tend to raise a red flag for the IRS, which could subject you to an audit.

One lawyer advised me to pay myself no more than $30,000 per year and simply take large draws. My CPA advised me to pay myself a defensible, fair market value salary, and then take reasonable draws from there. I followed my CPA's advice and, along with the advice from my CFO,[8] I take draws that are higher than my salary but I maintain a fair market value salary that is defensible despite my large draws.

When it comes to making these important decisions, find a CPA who is knowledgeable and trustworthy to advise you on the advantages and disadvantages of owner draws and salaries. Part of having a great business is having a team of professionals you can rely on to help guide you through decisions and evaluate the state of things in your firm.

When it comes to evaluating any decisions you make regarding the revenue in your law firm, there are two financial concepts to always keep in the forefront of your mind and business: taxes and core capital.

a. Taxes

Businesses are required to pay taxes on a quarterly basis. But the quarterly taxes you are paying are estimates based on your previous year's numbers. Have your CPA estimate your quarterly tax payments with the hope that you won't get stuck with a huge tax bill at the end of the year.

---

[8] In Step 5, "Streamlining Your Law Firm," I discuss the use of outside professional help to support you and help move your firm to the next level.

If you notice an uptick in revenue or if you project a revenue increase during the year, have your CPA adjust your estimated payments to avoid underpaying.

If you ever find yourself owing the IRS a hefty tax bill, the IRS offers payment plans, but it charges an insane amount of interest. You do not want the IRS to be your lender, which is how the book, *Simple Numbers, Straight Talk, Big Profits! 4 Keys to Unlock Your Business Potential*, puts it.[9] Instead, you want to be prepared.

I have done the tax scramble and it's awful. I once had trouble closing on a house because the mortgage company was requiring me to file my taxes by February 15 and pay in full the amount I owed, which was over $70,000. I owed because I had failed to adjust my quarterly tax payments to keep pace with the growth of my business. It was a terrible experience and one that I *do not* wish for you!

Be proactive when it comes to taxes. We have found that by putting away 20 percent of all the revenue we receive (in addition to our quarterly estimated payments), we are never in jeopardy of being unable to pay our taxes. If you do this and end up with funds left over at the end of the year, you'll have options of what to do with that savings. Most importantly, it means you won't have the IRS as your lender.

b. Core capital

The book, *Simple Numbers*, recommends a "core capital target" of two months of operating expenses and no debt. In order to calculate your core capital target, you need to know what all of your monthly operating expenses are. Once you've done that, place that money in an account labeled "Untouchable."

Will you be tempted to pull that money out as a dividend or draw? Yes. Will you think about all the fun things you could do with that

---

[9] *Simple Numbers, Straight Talk, Big Profits! 4 Keys to Unlock Your Business Potential*, by Greg Crabtree, can be found on Amazon at *https://www.amazon.com/dp/1608320561*.

money? Yes. Will you touch it? No. Why? You will need it in case of emergency. Things happen in life when you least expect it.

Case in point: My city and the surrounding areas suffered the effects of a severe snowstorm, shutting down everything for a week. That meant no new business at all during that time. But rent was still due. And so were all the other bills. Yet no money was coming in the door.

One week without any revenue is something that can completely cripple a business that is unprepared for it, and one month can make a business go bankrupt. Many of my colleagues in North Carolina and Texas were devastated by hurricanes—not only did they lose business, they suffered a lot of damage to offices and equipment. Without savings, going bankrupt could be the only option.

Tuck that money away so that you are prepared for any sort of unforeseeable event that could severely impact your business. Set yourself up for success by having some savings.

Once you have reached a place where you have no debt, you have at least two months of savings tucked away, and you have money put away for taxes, that is the time to consider taking an owner's draw or dividends.

What You Need to KNOW:

☐ ALL the work that must be done in a case in order to set an appropriate flat fee

☐ How to use engagement marketing to cultivate your existing clients

☐ The number and type of pro bono cases you will take each year

☐ What a lead is and how to cultivate it

☐ What your profit margin and P&L are

What You Need to DO:

☐ Increase your firm's business by setting the right fees for your services

☐ Implement a flat-fee structure for your firm

☐ Get paid in full up front. Try iQualify Lending.

☐ Sponsor your own free legal clinic

☐ Utilize existing networks for referrals

☐ Follow up on leads

☐ Pay yourself a fair market value salary

TAKING YOUR LAW FIRM'S BRAND TO THE NEXT LEVEL

"Are your clients seeing you the way you want to be seen?"

Sometimes, we need to stop and ask: What impression are we leaving our clients with? Unfortunately, the busier and more comfortable that we are in our businesses, the easier it is to miss things that are obvious to our clients.

As a result, we lose sight of the client experience.

Look around your office through your clients' eyes. What do you see? Is it a place that instills confidence or causes anxiety?

A messy desk, broken cabinets, phones that don't work properly, a ripped chair in the waiting room, a picture that hangs crooked. These items may seem insignificant in the grand scheme, but to your clients, they leave a lasting impression of you as a lawyer, a manager, even a person.

Assess your office surroundings as well as your own physical appearance. For example, over the years, I've noticed that the more burnt out I become, the more disheveled I become. I have gone to work with messy hair. I have even worn clothes that have made me look shabby; at times, they were too big or weren't even my style.

I put my looks last. The work was more important.

About six months after I had my baby, I wore to work a green and blue summer dress with black Toms. In hindsight, it was dreadful. My mom was visiting and asked, "Are you going to work like that?" I said, "Yes, I just had a baby—and if they have a problem with it then it's their problem."

But it was really *my* problem. I was overwhelmed but was afraid to admit it. While in denial, my physical appearance became the least of my concerns.

I was caught up in my business and lost myself along the way. I would never normally leave the house without makeup and my hair done. And to be seen in public wearing Toms? This was certainly not the Alexandra I knew—I love wearing high heels and fitted dresses. I realized I had to find myself again.

Maybe casual dress is part of your firm's culture. If so, then it's something you have implemented deliberately; it is how you want your clients to see you. But my choice of casual wear was not made consciously; it fell short of my own expectations. I wasn't giving it my best, which is my point.

Are your clients seeing you the way you want to be seen? Do you know what perception you want your clients to have of you? How can you ensure that you make the right first impression?

"Step 2: Taking Your Law Firm's Brand to the Next Level" is all about building the perception you want of yourself and your firm. It explains how to take deliberate steps toward choosing a business model that works for you and your clients; increasing your chances of being seen as a thought leader; creating a social media persona to attract more clients; creating ways to regularly communicate with clients to stay top of mind; and handling negative reviews from clients.

We will cover:

1. Branding Your Firm: Are You Walmart or Neiman Marcus?

2. Positioning Yourself as an Expert to Build Your Brand;
3. Using Facebook Live to Boost Your Firm's Brand and Presence;
4. Promoting Your Firm's Brand While Building an Email List;
5. Protecting Your Brand and Your Sanity; and
6. Responding to Bad Reviews.

Branding Your Firm: Are You Walmart or Neiman Marcus?

At the American Immigration Lawyers Association Solo and Small Firm Conference in December 2016, a speaker said something that made me take a harder look at my business.

He said, "Is your law firm a Walmart or is it a Neiman Marcus?" Which means, are you concerned with being the low cost leader? Or do your high prices reflect a high-value experience? Either way is fine, but either way must be intentional.

This sheds light on questions that are important for all solos and small firms to consider:

- Is it your business plan to have the lowest prices on the market? If so, there is absolutely nothing wrong with this. However, deciding to be the low-cost leader must be purposeful. Many solos and small firms end up with prices that are extremely low just because they don't feel empowered to charge more; or they feel bad about increasing their fee; or they feel afraid that they won't get clients without the low fee.

- If your prices are very low, ask yourself: "Do I want to be known as the low-cost attorney?"

- Would you prefer a practice with a lower number of cases that are priced higher?

There is a great deal of space between the extremes here, so it is important to find what feels right and works for you.

For example, when you are first starting out and you need to pay the bills, high volume for a lower amount could be the right solution for you. As your practice grows, your perspective on this may change.

There is no "right answer" for this. I worked for a well-established law firm that valued low, accessible prices and had high-volume as a business model. Bear in mind that the high-volume, low-cost model can lead to burnout. But only you know what's right for you and your business.

1. High-end vs. low-cost

Where does your firm fall on the Walmart/Neiman Marcus scale?

For many solos and small firms, we lean toward offering lower prices because we want to do it for the cause and not for the money.

Also, we are afraid that if we charge more, we would not have any new clients. We are afraid that people will walk away, so we price ourselves extremely low with the hope of landing the client.

For a long time, I was an accidental Walmart. I followed the low-cost model unintentionally. I didn't know how to set my fees, so I would undercharge and fail to bill. I was severely under-earning.

I had quality services and low prices, which meant that I needed to run a high-volume practice in order to survive. But this model had me drowning and always at the brink of a breakdown. I was not able to communicate with my clients as much as they wanted or needed.

When I finally broke free of the low-cost model, it allowed me to enhance my clients' experience exponentially and it also increased my income substantially.

2. High-end means added value

There is nothing wrong with operating like a Walmart. But if you'd rather be Macy's or Neiman Marcus, ask yourself: What additional value can you present to your clients to make the higher prices worth their while?

Neiman Marcus does everything high-end, from the brands it carries to its customer service. The sales associate will greet you, start a dressing room for you, and offer you bottled water and chocolates while you browse. These are small details but they make the customer feel welcome and pampered. It makes you feel like shopping there is well worth the expense.

My favorite restaurant offers a free glass of champagne to its patrons as they enter. We feel pampered every time we go. The brand of champagne isn't expensive, but it makes the experience feel very posh.

Small, thoughtful details can raise your firm's ambience. At the end of the day, the work you do is similar to the work performed by many other attorneys. What makes your firm stand out could be the "value-adds," which help create an atmosphere that makes the client feel pampered and special.

Try these:

- Offer bottles of water or a glass of water to everyone who comes in.

- Make available a menu of teas, coffees, and drinks.

- Provide a list of services included with your flat fee, such as in-house translations, notary services, client/attorney meetings, client/attorney phone calls, and more. By listing them out, the client perceives a higher value.

- Contact every client every month by letter or email.[1]

---

[1] "Step 4: It's All About the Client" provides additional guidance on how to stay in contact with your clients and nurture your relationships. See the section on Nurtur-

What do your clients want?

- Low prices?

- More nurturing?

- Dedicated attention?

By understanding what your clients want, it will help you determine price and also determine how to interact with your clients in a way that is meaningful for them.

When I decided to elevate my firm, I had to elevate it in every way. I had to make a shift in the presentation of my firm. I started by raising my fees in order to accept fewer clients. I hired additional help. I developed systems, standards, and policies as well as an employee manual and training guide.[2]

Everyone in my firm dresses in suit jackets when they meet with clients. We have formal scripts for greeting and handling client communication. This is because I considered my ideal client and what he or she would want and expect from a lawyer. I wanted to meet those expectations and then exceed them.

I realized that clients wouldn't mind paying more to have an elevated experience—more handholding, higher levels of communication, more sophistication in our contact, and more.

One time, a community "activist" came to my office and demanded to know why I charged more than another attorney in the area since we "do the same work." He wanted to refer people to me because he had heard good things about me, but he also wanted to refer people to the cheapest lawyer. I told him that being the cheapest isn't my business model. If people are searching for the cheapest lawyer, then my law firm may not be right for them.

---

ing Plus Over-communication: The Building Blocks of a Solid Attorney/Client Relationship.

[2] See my book, *Be the CEO of Your Law Firm: Gain Control, Turn a Profit, and Reclaim Your Life,* for detailed guidance on how to structure your law firm along with forms and documents to help you get started right away. Find it on Amazon at *https://www.amazon.com/dp/1732082502.*

Lesson Learned: Minimize confusion

For years, I had an internet-based phone for our firm's main number, but we could never get it to work properly. So we forwarded the number to the main desk phone, which had a completely different number. Clients could call in on the firm's main number, but we couldn't call out on it. And each desk phone had a different number associated with it, which meant that the clients were constantly getting calls from different numbers. Not one of these numbers was our firm's number. We even tried using a cell phone to call and text the firm's clients, but this number wasn't the firm's number either.

People were complaining that they had several numbers saved for us and never knew which number to use to contact us.

For a long time, I ignored the complaints because I was too caught up in the chaos of the business and the cases.

Finally, I brought in a business manager who straightened it out. He was able to streamline all of our communications through the one office number. The response from clients was amazing. They were happy to finally have calls and texts from one number.

Positioning Yourself as an Expert to Build Your Firm's Brand

Many attorneys desire to position themselves as experts in their chosen field of practice or niche, whether locally or nationally. The main ways to do this are through:

- Article publishing

- Media appearances

- Speaking engagements

- Peer recognition

1. Article publishing

Being a published author carries a certain amount of prestige and helps to position you as an expert in your field. Publishing articles in well-known periodicals can lead to public-speaking engagements, conference-panel participation, peer recognition, and, especially, additional clientele.

When writing an article, you have to determine who your audience will be. Are you writing for other lawyers to be recognized as an expert in your field? Or are you writing for clients so that they can understand elements of your area of practice better? They both require very different approaches.

a. Lawyers as your audience

When writing for lawyers, you might consider summarizing a recent court decision, a proposed piece of legislation, or even a regulation.

The article you want to write that interprets a new court decision is likely something that practitioners in your area of practice want to read and will find that your summary saves them from having to digest the case themselves.

When big things happen in my area of practice, I sometimes say, "Can someone break it down for me as if I were a fifth grader?" Well, you can be that person!

Not everyone has the passion or ability to understand a new law as it applies to your area of practice. Some writers have a knack for taking information, breaking it down into bite-size pieces, and empowering others to use that information to be better lawyers and to better serve their clients.

Bar publications are desperate for content and they need writers. Many bars have blogs in addition to their state bar publications. The same is true for specialty bars and federal bars. They *need* content. They *need* information. You can pitch them article ideas that will likely be accepted.

b. Potential clients as your audience

If you want to get in front of potential clients, find publications they read. Many publications are controlled by the news cycle, and they need to fill the space and are always looking for ways to accomplish that.

If you have an idea for an article, all you need to do is write to the publication—find the editor by doing a search on the website of the publication. It generally is easy to find.

Here is what you do:

- Choose a subject you would like to write about.

- Find five to 10 publications whose readers would be interested in that topic.

- Get the contact information for the editors of those publications.

- Save the information in a spreadsheet for future reference.

- Either outline the article or write it out so that it can be easily summarized for your pitch.

- Email each editor with the pitch.

- Use this template adapted from one of the top public relations experts in the world:

  Subject: Pitch- Summarize Story in 10 words or less (called "top line")

  Hi, first name,

  I was wondering if you would be interested in a story on (summary here/top line).

  2nd paragraph- what it is about, summary of idea.

  Look forward to hearing from you.

If you follow this format, and your article idea resonates with the editor, you will likely be published.

Eventually, you will cultivate a relationship with each editor so that you can have a go-to person for each idea you have and get on a list of whom to contact.

If you get published because of your pitching, then it means two things: (1) you are a great pitcher, and (2) you have something worth publishing!

Lesson Learned: What's the worst that could happen?

When I started pitching article ideas, I felt really embarrassed every time an article of mine was published. I felt shame. I felt like a fraud. I felt that if my writing and my ideas truly had any merit, I would have been published without having to ask for it.

But what was there to be ashamed of or embarrassed about? PR people do this all the time. They pitch to publishers of magazines, literary houses, even TV shows.

I realized that I'm no different from the people who pitch products to QVC. People are pitching to QVC so that their products can get on TV. If you have a product you want on QVC, you can't simply cross your fingers and pray that the QVC producers will find your website. Instead, you are going to be actively pitching as many times as it takes to get your product featured on the show!

What is the worst, most terrible, horrible, embarrassing, awful thing that could happen? They tell you they aren't interested. On an embarrassment scale of 1–10, writing a private email to someone about an article you wrote and receiving a response in a private email that the person isn't interested, rates about a 0.

It's not like the editor will take your email, publish it, and say, "Look at this crappy idea I received from Ally Lozano." That would be about a 10 on the embarrassment scale *and* it would never happen!

---

c. What about blogging?

Writing articles can include writing blogs; however, according to statistics I have heard and read, blogs only generate business at a rate of 1 percent. This means that whether you write daily, weekly, or monthly, your blog will only have a 1 percent return on investment.

As a solo practitioner, your two most precious resources are money and time, so anything that has a 1 percent return is not worth your money or your time. You could find more lucrative avenues than a blog.

Here's the thing about a lawyer blog: most of the topics that are interesting to you as an attorney or relate to your area of practice are not interesting to anyone other than those in your field.

For example, an article about how to spot a loophole in a contract for a merger and acquisition is absolutely uninteresting to anyone except for someone who reads contracts for a living. Any company that is doing a merger and acquisition will have a lawyer who reads the contract; no one in the company will need to do that.

Therefore, if you are an attorney who works with mergers and acquisitions, you would be writing that article essentially for yourself.

Do you get what I am saying?

However, that article may be interesting to other people who practice in your area of law. In fact, it could be a great article to have published in a periodical for your specific practice area, and then post an announcement to your website under "Bar News for Mergers and Acquisitions Lawyers."

You can include the link to the article and promote the link, *not* because your clients and potential clients want to read the article, but because they want to see you featured as an expert somewhere.

However, offering basic, simple, and easy-to-read information on your website in the form of short articles, preferably bullet-pointed, is a great idea. It wouldn't be a blog; it would be an "Information You Need to Know" section.

As an example, many of my immigration clients think they can gain legal status through their children. Unfortunately, the majority cannot. We created a one-page handout called, "Why Can't I Get My Papers Based on My Kids?" Clients like it because it's easy to read and they can reference it often. This is also an example of a "blog post" that my clients actually *want* and *need* and can access the information from my website.

The same can work for maintaining any social media pages. Share information that your potential clients want or need to know. For example, the details or fact pattern of a groundbreaking case might not be worthwhile to your clients, but if the outcome impacts your clients' cases, you have the perfect opportunity to explain in a blog post what the case means to them.

The *why* does not matter, only the *how* and the *what* are important. The clients want to know *how* the change impacts their situation, for better or for worse. And *what* the next steps are.

2. Media appearances

Media outlets need something new, fresh, and current pretty much all the time, and they are desperate to fill their time slots. Why not fill them with you?

Try the following:

- Identify a few newspapers, radio stations, and/or TV stations that could cover something related to you, your work, and/or your mission.

- Find the producer of the TV segment or the newspaper section that would be most appropriate for your theme.

- Write a pitch to the producer or editor.

- Follow up in about three days if you haven't heard back (they are very busy).

- If they want to cover your story, create about three main points that you want to convey in your interview. *No matter what they ask, bring it back to your talking points*! It is all about getting your message across. It is easy to get caught up in their questions, but you are the expert and you are there for a reason—to present *your* point of view about *your* case/work/mission.

Here are two makeup tips I have learned for appearing on TV:

(1) Do a strong lip – the lighting will wash out your face and a strong lip helps you stand out more.

(2) Use contour to shape your face. Put a lot of it along your jaw line and also along the lines on your cheeks that are made when you suck in your cheeks (think of making a "fishy face"). It will help you look thinner. Yes, I deeply care about this! I even have asked the producers to shoot me from different angles that I know will make my face look thinner—for example, from higher up and angled. Hey, if I am going to be on TV, I want to look my best!

I had been on TV before, but I had never been on TV as an expert in a case that I was personally working on.

I took over a case where the client already had gone to the media about her situation. Her daughter's teacher found out what was happening to my client, and was so outraged that she picked up the phone and called the local TV station to tell them about it. Once that station got involved, the other local stations wanted to cover the story as well as the local newspapers, both print and digital.

I knew that with the media, I had to meet two objectives: (1) paint my client's story in the way that I wanted it to be perceived so that it would support our legal theory; and (2) position myself as an expert for future news stories.

For part 1, I laid out three talking points that I wanted to convey to the media—both from my client's perspective and mine. I practiced over and over with her, and when she said something outside of the talking points that I felt wouldn't support the story we wanted to present, I asked the person filming to reshoot that part or to edit it out.

For part 2, I got the card of every single person who interviewed me, and I also gave them my email address so they could email me with follow-up questions. I asked them to email me when an article ran or with a replay of the news clip.

I followed up with a thank-you email for giving my client the opportunity to share her story and how much I appreciated the coverage. I said that if they ever needed someone to speak on immigration issues or to give an opinion about an immigration event, they could always reach out to me.[3]

After that email, I sent a gift box of cookies to each person who interviewed me. One of them said she couldn't accept it because she had to be unbiased in her reporting but told me she was going to donate it to a homeless shelter for mothers and children. I am sure that even though she couldn't keep it, she will remember the gesture.

And just like that, I have a personal media contact in every local media station—both newspaper and TV. It was that easy!

About a month later, I had an urgent case, so I went to one of my media contacts and said, "I have an urgent case, here's the summary—can you cover this?" This was at 6:00 pm on a Thursday. He immediately replied and said that the Friday slots for news were filled, but they wanted to air it on the prime time news on Monday. By Friday at 10:00 am, my client and I were both slated for interviews and his story aired just as promised on the Monday news.

There is *no* reason why you cannot do this, too.

3. Speaking engagements

Just like legal publications, legal conferences are desperate for speakers. Some are five days long and they need to have tons of topics and speakers to fill the time. Why couldn't you be one of them?

If there is a call for speakers, be sure to respond. Say that you can speak on a range of topics, and highlight three to five different topics that you could speak on. Also, since most of these conferences love panels, it's a great idea to propose an entire panel of speakers that can speak to a certain topic or area of law—this will make it easier for them to choose you.

---

[3] You can also list yourself for free on the website, *Help a Reporter Out*. You'll receive media opportunities via email. If you upgrade to a subscription, you'll have more control over the types of inquiries you receive and you can create a profile on the site.

Planning conferences is a huge undertaking; and by making these proposals, it makes it much easier for the planning committee. In turn, it will help you get selected!

Again, the worst that can happen is that they say no—and again, it is pretty low on the embarrassment scale.

Take action now:

- Find upcoming events in your local or national bar association or organization that are in line with your expertise.

- Research the contact information of the person/people who are organizing the event.

- Propose three to five topics that you can speak on and/or panels that you could put together.

- Be sure to follow up. Many lawyers who are planning events also are working full time as lawyers, and your email may get lost in their inbox.

Lesson Learned: You can nominate yourself

I remember as a young lawyer, I dreamt of the day that I would be asked to speak on a panel in my area of law. I remember thinking that, one day, I would be "expert enough" that people would want to listen to what I have to say about immigration law.

As I got involved in the governance of my local immigration law chapter, I quickly realized that the people who got speaking opportunities were the ones who asked for them. I had some illusion in my head that someone needed to write in about me so that I would be chosen. Then I found out that people wrote in to suggest themselves!

Of course, in my youthful ignorance, I thought, "How could they do that? Who do they think they are?" Yes, I judged them—and that's because it was a judgment of my own self. Why did I think that I was *not* good enough to be there? Why didn't I think of offering my own voice?

The more you speak, the more you will be asked because your name will be out there.

4. Peer recognition

Remember what I said about pitching articles? People aren't picked for articles and news stories out of the blue. They are picked because they pitch (or someone pitches on their behalf). Understand that no one out there who is a featured expert is any better than you are as an attorney; they are exactly the same as you. All they did was make the phone call, send the email, or whatever it took to get their voices heard.

Now, what if I told you that the same is true for awards? The odds are extremely low that someone will see an award and think of you. This means that in order to get an award, it's not about being discovered, it's about finding the award and then finding a way to get nominated for it.

Most of the time, you can't nominate yourself. However, you can ask someone to nominate you. Likely, you have a close friend or colleague who knows you and your work well. You can write to the friend and send a link to the award and ask if he or she would be willing to nominate you for the award. You can send a summary of why you think you would be a good candidate for the award and also offer to do all the paperwork.

I challenge you to research awards in your area of practice and consider yourself for the nomination. What's required? Why do you think you would be the right fit?

List all the reasons why you would be the right person. Then don't be shy about asking your colleagues to support you.

Lesson Learned: Let people know

I have a close colleague who has been an incredible mentor to me and to others. She is a giving, kind person who has constantly answered emails, shared legal arguments, and supported colleagues when things have been challenging.

So you would think that when a mentoring award was announced, she would have instantly popped into my mind. Nope. Not even for a moment. And the ironic thing is that I wanted to nominate someone I knew for the award because I had won that award in the past. When I saw the email announcing the award, I opened it, thought to myself, "I want to nominate someone I know for this award. Okay, Ally, don't forget to do that." And then I deleted the email and forgot about it.

A few weeks later, I got a message from the associate attorney who works for the attorney whom I mentioned above, and she asked whether I would be willing to nominate her boss for the award.

In that moment it clicked. I wrote, "YES, YES, YES! I would LOVE to nominate her!!!" If her associate attorney hadn't reached out to me, I would likely have never thought about it.

Once I announced to the members of my international network of female immigration attorneys that I wanted to nominate her, about 100 people wrote in to support the nomination. That's how loved she is. That's how appropriate it was for her to be nominated. Yet, her nomination almost did not happen simply because everyone who would've nominated her was so busy living her own life and focusing on her own to-do list. That is why there is power in asking to be nominated.

The great news is she won the award! It was an important milestone for her and her career.

Using Facebook Live to Boost
Your Firm's Brand and Presence

Facebook, as well as other social media, provides an opportunity for you to have a conversation with potential clients. On a website, your potential clients don't really get to interact with you. On social media, people have the opportunity to get to know you.

And there is no better way to do this than through Facebook Live!

Facebook Live is a live broadcast from your firm's Facebook page, which allows you to speak with your followers via chat. When you "go live," Facebook will notify your followers that you are live so that people can log in, watch you speak, and post comments and questions.

I decided to use Facebook Live similar to a radio show—essentially, I go live and encourage people to ask me questions and I answer them right there. I call my show, *Mi Abogada Dice*®, and people love it. They ask questions, and I get to respond immediately in real time. I offer a discount to participants who decide to schedule a consultation.

One advantage to using Facebook Live is that the video you create continues to exist on your Facebook page, so people will continue to "like" and comment on it as the days and weeks go by. It brings a lot of interaction to your page, and it is a great way to get more followers and more people engaged with you, your work, and your mission. More people are able to get a feel for who you are as a person and as an attorney, which can help them build confidence in you and your firm.

Facebook Live is completely different from uploading a pre-recorded video. Most pre-recorded videos are short, less than 90 seconds. But Facebook Live requires 15 minutes or longer to build an audience.

I absolutely love Facebook! That's where I have found my ideal client.[4] Regardless of who your ideal client is, it is likely that he or she is on Facebook. I recommend that you get on Facebook right away to get more clients.

1. Prepare in advance

You can host your Facebook Live show at a specific time every week to answer questions live. This has been incredibly successful for every lawyer I know who has tried it.

At first, you may not get any questions, so you might want to have some talking points planned. Avoid legalese and try not to over-explain things. Use the words that your clients would use. Break it down in a way that non-lawyers will understand. For example, every-

---

[4] Get help developing your ideal client with tips and exercises outlined in chapter 1 of my book, *Be the CEO of Your Law Firm: Gain Control, Turn a Profit, and Reclaim Your Life.*

one uses the word "divorced," so instead of saying, "When filing for marriage dissolution," you would say, "When filing for a divorce." Make your language accessible and easy to understand.

Also, make it high energy and entertaining. I have seen some attorneys talk in such a technical way or monotone, making their live broadcast boring to watch and listen to. You want to get people excited about interacting with you.

Because a lot of people have never worked with a lawyer before, you could start by explaining what it is you do for your clients or how a typical case is handled.

So many lawyers are afraid to use Facebook Live because they will look bad or make a mistake, or that someone might leave a negative comment. If those things do happen, it's not a big deal. You can always delete the videos if you don't like them, and you can delete negative comments or block the person who left the comment.

My followers are so happy that I am available to answer their questions, alleviate their fears, and put a voice to the lawyer they are considering investing in, both financially and emotionally. Your followers will feel the same way.

Facebook Live is a tremendous business development tool and I really encourage you to try it.

2. Consistency is required

Facebook, including Facebook Live, is a marathon and not a sprint. A lot of people will be following you on Facebook for a while before they pick up the phone to call you. That's why it is important to be consistent.

The majority of my business comes from Facebook, and it's because of consistency. I have had people say to me, "I have been watching your page for two years just waiting for the right time to come in to see you." Other clients have said, "I was just waiting for you to post about a case that sounded like mine, and then you did, so I knew I could trust you."

Use Facebook Live consistently for six months and you will see results. It doesn't require much of your time and it is completely free, unless you choose to run paid advertisements. You will make yourself stand out in the market.

Follow these tips to get started:

- Pick a day and go live on that day every week. People will get to know your schedule.

- Name your show.

- Create an image based on the theme for the show. Add it in the description so that people can see it when you go live. If you use an image from the internet, use only non-copyrighted, royalty-free images. There are many websites that offer images you can use for free or for a small fee, such as canva.com, pixabay.com, unsplash.com, istock.com, and shutterstock.com.

- Create a meme for your show. Memes are just pictures with text on them. These are often better than pictures you grab from the web because you can brand them; you can add your firm name and number, an email address, a hashtag, and more. It's also a great way for people to save your contact info for later.

- Open your show by introducing yourself. For example, "I'm Alexandra Lozano, the lead attorney of Alexandra Lozano Immigration Law, and I am here to answer your questions about immigration. If you have any questions, please leave them in the comments below so I can answer them live. Also, if you would like to speak to me privately and schedule a consultation, call my office at ___-__-____. Don't forget that I am here to answer your questions live, so write your questions in the comments below."

- Discuss one of your main case types. For example, "Have you ever worked for an employer who refused to pay you overtime? If so, you may qualify for _____." Then review the basics of the legal remedies and how you can help.

- Respond to questions from your audience.

- Give general legal information. Avoid giving advice that is too specific. Use their questions to discuss the law generally; that way, people who are watching can somewhat "self-analyze" to see if the information applies to them.

- Use a disclaimer at the beginning and remind viewers that you are providing only legal information, not legal advice, and that for individualized legal advice, they can schedule a consultation.

- Always tell participants to call for an appointment for more specific information. If a question is overly complicated, give some short, general information followed by an explanation that the specifics really require and deserve an in-person consultation.

- Always remind people to call your office. Repeat the phone number several times throughout the broadcast and suggest a consultation.

- "Like" every comment you get and draft a canned response to comments. An example would be, "Thank you for giving me the opportunity to answer your question today on my show!" Then include your phone number again.

- Respond to private messages with a canned response and suggest a consultation. Your goal is to turn browsers into buyers. *See below for an example of a canned response.*

- Plan on doing a 30-minute live broadcast. In general, 30 minutes is the most effective amount of time.

- Have some questions already drafted just in case you don't receive any from your audience.

- Consider paying Facebook to boost your video for a broader response.

3. Using canned responses

As you build your business page, you will begin to receive private messages asking you very specific questions and expecting free advice. Do not get trapped by this. Instead, create a canned response to these questions, such as:

> Thank you so much for your question. Your case interests me and I would love to give you the time that you deserve to discuss this in more detail. The best step here would be to schedule a one-hour, in-person consultation with me. Our number is _____, so feel free to give us a call.

If you run your business page correctly, you will be empowering your followers with lots of great, free information—informative videos, your Facebook Live show, and regular updates.

But the other purpose of your page is to build your business. Your goal, then, is to turn browsers into buyers. I often say that the way to make Facebook fail for you is to spend your time answering requests for free information. And you wouldn't want to be viewed as having started an attorney/client relationship where there really is none.

A colleague of mine has a very successful Facebook page. She is able to collect people's phone numbers, and her receptionist follows up with each person by calling him or her. She has found that to be a successful strategy for turning those browsers into buyers.

Promoting Your Brand While Building an Email List

There is a right way and a wrong way to build an email list. The wrong way is to simply purchase some generic list of email addresses without really knowing whether they fit your ideal client profile. Not only is this a waste of time and money for you, but it could also cause you to be blocked by your email service provider if people report your emails as spam, block you, or unsubscribe.

The right way to go about building an email list is the old fashioned, organic way—through personal contact with those you come across while networking, speaking, or engaging on a professional level. In-person events are the best way to promote your services and your brand.

Here are a few ways to promote your brand while collecting email addresses of those who are interested in what you offer:

- *Use a sign-up sheet*: At trade shows and community events, collect email addresses using a sign-up sheet for your email newsletter.

- *Collect business cards*: Whether you're attending a trade show, community event, or networking event, always ask for a business card and offer yours. If you are exhibiting, set out a glass bowl, gift bag, or basket to collect business cards for a raffle or giveaway. On the back of your business card, you can include an offer to encourage people to visit your website and sign up for your newsletter.

- *Host an event*: Host or sponsor an event that will provide you with the attendees' contact information. Make sure the event is well-branded with your firm's name and logo on all marketing materials, emails, and signs. Provide goodie bags with items branded with your firm's name, *i.e.*, pens, mugs, post-it notes, notebooks, phone screen wipes, hand sanitizer, etc.

- *Connect with people on social media*: You will have access to the email addresses of your connections on social media. But before you add them to your email list, kindly ask for permission first, as many of your connections may not wish to be arbitrarily added.

- *End social media posts with a call to action*: Whenever you post content to social media—be it video, text, or an article link—always include a call to action that prompts your reader to visit your website to complete a contact form. Make sure your social media posts are branded with your firm's name, logo, and contact information.

- *Attend networking events*: Join your local chamber of commerce and other business networking groups. Collect their business cards and follow up via email to share more information about your services.

- *Include an opt-in form on your website*: Whenever someone visits your website, never let the person go without at least providing a sign-up form to promote your firm's newsletter. Place a sign-up form on every page that a visitor would typically visit.

- *Offer a freebie*: Maybe you have a list of FAQs or an article that explains a common scenario, or a "know your rights" summary that you can use to entice people to sign up to download the item for free. Offering something in exchange for their contact information is more likely to convince visitors to opt in. Be sure to include your firm's name, logo, and contact information on every document you prepare as a freebie to attract clients.

- *Include a link in your email signature*: Your email signature should include a link to a sign-up page. Use it to promote your newsletter or an FAQ.

Building an email list is critical to your firm's longevity. It's great to have hundreds or thousands of followers or connections on social media, but if social media were to disappear tomorrow, where would you be? Start developing your own contact list today.

Protecting Your Brand and Your Sanity

Lawyers are pretty public nowadays whether we want to be or not. We have websites and social media pages that allow people to leave comments. We are listed on websites that rank us based on the reviews we receive from people. Lawyers today are treated similar to restaurants—everywhere you look, you'll find reviews of lawyers mixed in with reviews on eateries, products, and hotels.

Many attorneys resist posting videos on social media because they think people won't like the video, or someone will find fault with what's being said by the attorney, or that people will post cruel comments. All of these things can and do happen.

So what can you do when haters happen?

When someone speaks negatively about you—whether it's a bad review on a website, or an attack posted on your Facebook page, or a mean email—it hurts. Emotionally, it knocks you down. One negative comment can ruin an entire day—or week or month!

That fear-based voice in your mind hijacks your brain and starts attacking you. You obsess over it non-stop.

But the more you obsess over it, the more into the depths of obsession you go, and the more it consumes your very existence. You start to question yourself and your judgment.

Maybe someone has accused you of conducting yourself unprofessionally in your dealings with that person.

You start to question yourself.

> "Did I do a bad job for her?"

> "Was I untruthful in some way?"

> "Did I mislead her as to the outcome of her case?"

> "Do other people think this about me?"

> "What if other lawyers see it?"

> "What if potential clients see it?"

So how can you handle it? Below are three steps to help you combat the hurt feelings and negative thoughts, and remain focused on what is still most important.

1. Remember that haters are the minority voice

The funny thing about negativity is that it tends to overshadow all the positivity that came before it. You could have 100 positive, five-star reviews—talking about how amazing you are, the great results you accomplished for your clients, and more—and then you get the one negative comment that rocks your whole world.

It is impossible that every single person who ever comes into contact with you will be a person who absolutely loves you. And while we know this, it's still difficult to handle the one gut-punching comment.

When a hater gets you down, remember how many positive comments you've received before you received that one negative comment. Think about how many people love and support you. Keep reminding yourself that the hater is the minority voice.

Use this to "talk back" to those negative thoughts and calm your mind before it gets out of control. But if your mind is already spinning, you can use it to help neutralize the threat.

2. Honor the hater

Sounds crazy, right? But a hater is an opportunity to look inward. This doesn't mean that you agree with the comment, but it does give you a chance to examine yourself and the situation to look for ways to improve.

The person who is writing the comment about you is writing from his or her perspective. We can honor that even if we don't agree with it. While the words may sting and the comment may be unkind, I always take a moment to send that person a good thought or good energy.

Then, with an open mind, dissect the comment. What can you learn or improve from this?

All negative comments should not be treated equally. Just because someone says something negative about you doesn't mean it's true or that it has any merit. It doesn't mean that you can or should do anything better or differently. It doesn't mean that you must make a change.

Consider a negative comment akin to feedback rather than an attack. Look for the constructive aspects that may be buried between the hurtful words.

I begrudgingly admit that I have one negative review online. If you Google me, you will see it. He went to every website and left a negative review—Google, Avvo, Yelp, you name it.

While I don't agree with his perspective on the situation, I had some takeaways. For example, I told him I would get back to him once I looked something up, but it took me a week to do that. Realistically, I probably could have had the answer in about 24 hours, but I believe one week is reasonable.

And while I believe one week is reasonable, I decided that I wanted to take a deeper look at this. I used it as an opportunity to change something within myself. I decided from that point on, when I have a consultation and I need to get back to the person, I will do so within 24 hours—even if it's just to say that I need a little more time.

I should've followed my instincts and refused the case. The type of case wasn't my strongest and he gave off all the signs of a high-maintenance client. I eventually made a qualified referral to another attorney whom I thought would be right for the case, but he was unhappy with that.

Looking back, I see how I could have handled the situation better. He says that I told him I was too busy, which is not what I said; however, that's how he heard it. I should have expressed myself more clearly when talking about how and why I needed to refer his case.

3. Put on your hater headphones

After you have worked through steps 1 and 2, throw those hater headphones on and move forward.

At the end of the day, you have a special gift that the world needs. No one can do what you do the way that you do it. You have to keep shining your light and bringing forth the gifts you possess.

The most important thing you can do is to *not* let it bring you down or slow your progress. It would be easy to give up—to shut down your social media page, stop doing Facebook Live, or stop putting out your content. This is especially true when you have multiple people hating on you at once.

Lesson Learned: Be ok with not being liked by everyone

There have been moments when I considered stopping my consulting work with other attorneys because of negative comments and nasty things that people have said to me or about me. But my desire to serve and help lawyers build practices and lives that they love is greater than any negative comment.

The people I serve through my law firm or through my consulting are more important to me than the voice of anyone who expresses dislike with my message, my voice, or my mission.

I, of course, wallow in those moments and I go through the steps I have highlighted here. But I remind myself of the people who support me and who have benefited from my work, and take time to reflect on how I can improve. Then, I throw on those headphones and keep moving forward.

You aren't going to be everyone's cup of tea. And that is okay.

Below is a very detailed outline of ways to proactively combat bad reviews on online. Taking these steps will help preserve your reputation, your brand, and your sanity.

4. Combat bad reviews with good reviews

Ask your client for a review after you have concluded working on a case. Here's a sample email:

> Subject Line: Congratulations + Favor
>
> Dear _____, congratulations on the resolution of your legal matter! (You can be more specific here) It has been a pleasure working with you over the past _____ months/ years. I am proud to have been able to obtain this great result for you.
>
> I have a favor to ask. Would you be willing to leave me a review on Google and also on Avvo? Your perspective and insight will serve many people who are going through this process and

aren't sure where to turn. On Google, you can just google "[firm name]" and then click on "write a review." You can leave a review on Avvo by clicking here: [link to direct site].

I appreciate your time and consideration in this request. Thank you!

Sincerely,
[lawyer name]

Send out surveys to gather testimonials and also insight on how to make your firm better.

Responding to Bad Reviews

a. Do not attack back
b. Be very careful to not reveal privileged information
c. Be as diplomatic as possible
d. Example responses:

> We're sorry you had a bad experience with our firm. This matter does not sound familiar, and we strive for the utmost in client satisfaction in every case. Please contact me directly to discuss your specific concerns.

> Or

> Our firm is dedicated to the highest level of customer service. It appears that you are unhappy with the service that you received, which is something that we take very seriously. Please contact our office because we would like to make working with our firm a positive experience for you.

Handling Fake Reviews:

Google

1. Flag a review in your account for removal.
2. The review will be assessed and possibly removed from your listing.
3. Google also has a phone number you can call.

a. How to: Desktop

4. Sign in to Google My Business.
5. If you have two or more listings, switch to card view and click Manage location for the location you'd like to manage.
6. Click Reviews from the menu.
7. Find the review you'd like to flag, click the three dot menu then click Flag as inappropriate.

b. How to: Mobile

8. Open the Google My Business app.
9. Tap the menu ☰ , then tap Reviews.
10. Find the review you'd like to flag, tap the three-dot menu then tap Flag review.

Google Maps

11. Open Google Maps.
12. Find your business listing.
13. Find the review you'd like to flag.
14. Click the three dot menu then click Flag as inappropriate.
15. Like all of the positive reviews.
16. Request positive reviews from clients and colleagues.
17. Ask the clients and colleagues to "like" the positive reviews.
18. Ask the clients and colleagues to flag the fake review.

19. Keep flagging the bad review! Over and over and over!

Avvo

a. Post a response to the review

There is a link at the bottom of each review for you to post a response. Your comment will be displayed immediately below the disputed review, and the most effective responses to negative feedback online can be a simple comment. This also sends a powerful message to potential clients about your professionalism and interest in resolving any issues.

b. Request that the review be put through the dispute process

If you believe the review did not come from an actual or potential client of yours, Avvo will contact the reviewer and ask that person to confirm that he or she was in fact a real or potential client and give the person the option to edit or delete the review. During the dispute, the review will not appear on your profile. If the reviewer responds and confirms the review, it will be reposted to your profile with any changes specified by the reviewer.

Facebook

You can report reviews that do not follow the Facebook Community Standards or do not focus on the product or service offered by the Page. Facebook reviews your report and may remove reviews that do not follow its guidelines. You can only report star ratings that include reviews.

a. To report a review:

1. Go to the review and click ••• in the top right.
2. Click Report post.

3. Follow the on-screen instruction.

b. Contact reviewer/firm directly

4. Check the reviewer's profile to see if the person's employment is listed.
5. If the reviewer is from another firm, contact the attorney to discuss.

c. Turn off reviews

Yelp

a. Request a review to be removed

There are three main reasons why Yelp might remove a review:

1. <u>The reviewer has an apparent conflict of interest</u>

○ They appear to be a competitor or former employee
○ They appear to be affiliated with the business
○ They're receiving payment or other incentives for the review
○ They're promoting the business of a competitor

2. <u>The review doesn't focus on the reviewer's own consumer experience</u>

○ It's about someone else's consumer experience
○ It's a response to a current event in the news
○ It's primarily disputing another Yelper's review
○ It's about a different business
○ It appears to be plagiarized from another source

3. <u>The review includes inappropriate material</u>

○ It contains hate speech, lewd commentary, or threatening language
○ It contains private information about employees or patrons

b. How to report the review

1. Claim your business page.
2. Locate the review in the Reviews section of your business account.
3. Find the flag icon and click Report this review.

What You Need to KNOW:

☐ What type of business plan you want for your firm and what will work in your market

☐ What publications your ideal clients read and engage with

☐ The types of awards you want to be nominated for and whether you meet the criteria

☐ How to be consistent in your approach to social media

☐ You cannot please everyone and that haters are the minority

What You Need to DO:

☐ Choose a business model that works for you and your clients

☐ Utilize ways to increase your visibility and become a thought leader

☐ Incorporate Facebook Live into your social media strategy

☐ Create different ways to communicate with your clients

☐ Address negative reviews in a professional manner

CONQUERING SALES WITH CONFIDENCE AND AUTHENTICITY

"The art of selling also teaches us how to nurture and interact with clients."

You might be surprised to find a section covering sales in this book, and maybe you're saying, "Why do I need to know about sales when I'm a lawyer?"

Well, what if I told you that you *are* a salesperson? What would you think?

You *are* a salesperson because you sell a service. And in order to reach higher levels of success, you need to master some of the sales basics.

As attorneys, we are selling our services. Our expertise. Our knowledge. Our education.

Selling all of these things leads to a return on our investment—years spent in law school, years spent honing our logical and reasoning skills, and years spent gaining real-world legal practice experience.

Like every business, whether selling products or services, getting paid is the "reward" for providing a great product or service.

But where is the value in what we do as lawyers?

Take my immigration law practice, for example. I get green cards (or lawful permanent residency) for some of my clients, and being able to do that provides immense value to my clients. Gaining lawful residence in the United States means they have stability and security. They have a way to seek work so they can provide for themselves and their families as well as future generations. What I deliver to them is life-changing.

Yet for years, my fees were extremely low, especially on cases I thought were easy. When I heard that other lawyers charged more, I was incredulous. I thought, "How could they charge so much for the exact same thing that I do?" I even felt like I was somehow "better" than they were because I charged less when they charged more. I felt that my prices showed that I cared more somehow.

So many of us make the mistake of judging others when all they are doing is charging based on their value. We are quick to judge them because it shows how much we are failing to value ourselves.

In essence, if a person has a legal problem, any good lawyer can fix it. But you aren't just any good lawyer—you are *you*. You have something that makes you stand out from the crowd. Only you can do what you do in the way that you do it.

"Step 3: Conquering Sales with Confidence and Authenticity" describes how to incorporate sales techniques by focusing on the value you provide to your clients; how to quote your pricing without feeling uneasy; how to focus your responses on the questions clients need answered and to be prepared to overcome objections; how to incorporate visuals to help explain a complicated process; and how to present additional services to keep the client relationship going.

We will cover:

1. Incorporating a Sales Presentation into Your Consultation Without Sounding Salesy;
2. Incorporating Value-Based Quoting into Your Consultations;

3. Overcoming Objections; and
4. Creative Upselling.

Incorporating a Sales Presentation into Your Consultation Without Sounding Salesy

When I first started learning about sales, I said, "This isn't for me," and, "This doesn't relate to lawyers." But it does! Selling is all about expressing to clients *why* they need *your* services in particular and the *value* they will derive from having used *your* services.

The art of selling for lawyers isn't really as much about selling as it is about making the client feel comfortable. When a client feels comfortable with you, he or she is more inclined to trust you with his or her problem.

Your objectives are to listen well, allow the person to speak, and then offer a plan in a well thought-out presentation that makes the complicated part of hiring a lawyer seem simple and not so scary.

When you think of sales in this way, it becomes more palatable.

A sales presentation isn't some slimy pitch meant to sell a potential client on something that he or she doesn't need. Instead, a sales presentation can articulate what it is that you do, how you do it, and why the client needs it.

1. A good sales technique can simplify your consultation

A consultation is a sales presentation. When you approach your consultation from a sales perspective, you will be able to give your clients the maximum amount of information in the easiest way for them to understand.

Lawyers have a way of overexplaining things. We explain all the complexities of the case and walk the client through a point-by-point legal analysis. While this analysis might be interesting stuff for lawyers who practice in your field, it is way over the heads of clients. This includes clients who are lawyers but may not be familiar with your practice area.

When clients come to you for consultation, they want to know if you can solve their problem. They want to know how long it will take. And they want to know the cost. That's it.

Clients don't want to know the details of how you will solve their problem. Ironically, that's what attorneys spend the most time on during a consultation.

2. A good sales technique creates an environment of good customer service

One of the "basics" of sales is to regularly use someone's name when you speak with him or her. For example, we repeat a person's name at least three times during a phone interaction. It helps the person feel acknowledged. We apply that sales principle to family members as well. We ask about a family member, and we refer to him or her by name.

The art of selling also teaches us how to nurture and interact with clients. If someone gets married, has a baby, graduates, and the like, we send a small gift and card. We send a small branded gift when someone signs a contract with us. We "spoil" our clients by making what is important to them important to us.[1]

3. A good sales technique allows you to make a living

Let's face it. If you are not getting consultations or new cases signed up, then you cannot make a living. By using sales techniques,

---

[1] "Step 4: It's All About the Client" provides additional guidance on how to nurture your clients to enhance the client experience. See the section on Nurturing Plus Over-communication: The Building Blocks of a Solid Attorney/Client Relationship.

you can help a client understand the value that you provide, what makes you different from anyone else, and the unique way that you will handle the case (not just legally but on a personal level).

Most lawyers cringe at the thought of sales. We think of a person who is slimy and dishonest. We certainly don't think that any sales concepts should apply to us, those who are out there doing the important, life-changing work that we do.

However, we are wrong. The fact that we do important, life-changing work is precisely why we need to incorporate sales techniques into what we do.

Instead of focusing on all the things that you want to talk about and what you want the client to know, you must focus on answering the client's questions with the most important, relevant information.

Here are a few more reasons why sales techniques are important:

- You offer a service to a client in a way that no one else does. Though you may provide the same legal services as other attorneys, the personal and professional way that you do it is unique.

- You have personal motivations for why you do this work.

- You know the legal process from beginning to end.

- You can offer the client a solution that will solve the problem that he or she has.

Here's the catch—most lawyers do not communicate any of these reasons to their clients. This is precisely the information that clients and potential clients need to hear from lawyers.

Let's break it down. There are four questions that a potential client needs answered during a consultation:

1. Can you help me?
2. How long will it take?
3. How much will it cost?
4. What do you need from me?

It is your job to answer those four questions, *plus* show why *you* are the right lawyer to handle the case.

You must plan a way to speak directly and concisely to those four questions—that's what sales is all about!

I have had to work with lawyers for different reasons. I've used a personal-injury attorney and an estate-planning attorney. I currently retain an IP attorney, and I work with an employment attorney from time to time when I have questions about employee-related issues.

The ones I enjoy working with speak simply and clearly. Just because I am a lawyer doesn't mean I understand their practice area, so I need them to break it down to me in the most basic way so that I can understand.

Exercise: Write Your Sales Pitch

Answer the following questions, and then put your answers together in a short summary. Practice communicating this to your clients and incorporate it into your consultations.

Why should a client hire you?

_____

_____

_____

_____

What do you do differently from other law firms?

_____

_____

_____

_____

Why do you do this work?

_____

_____

_____

_____

What personal experiences have you had that inspire the work that you do?

_____

_____

_____

_____

What results have you gained for clients of which you are most proud?

_____

_____

_____

_____

What is an easy to understand, non-legalese summary of the legal process?

_____

_____

_____

_____

What are the benefits of this process in particular to the client?

_____

_____

_____

_____

What results can your client expect to have from you? When?

_____

_____

_____

_____

How can your services change your client's life?

_____

_____

_____

_____

4. A good sales technique includes handouts and visuals

The best way to conduct a sales presentation is with written material that you can use during your consultation.

I explain the big concepts with handouts. Clients _love_ it. Some people even say, "No one ever explained it this way to me before, thank you so much."

From the client's perspective, things are much clearer!

From the lawyer's perspective, all the information has been presented to the client, including the price. The written materials help present the price to the client in the benefits part of the presentation.

Have you ever been to a sales presentation for a new home or condo? They usually have a scaled model to show you what it will look like. They even have 3D models online. They provide you a brochure or folder filled with beautiful pictures of all the amenities that the new complex will have. By the time you leave there, you are imagining yourself immersed in the luxury that the condo or home promises.

This is because they have helped you see and understand the whole picture, even when construction hasn't started yet.

When it comes to a legal process, it is harder for potential clients to picture it in their heads from beginning to end, and it can't be presented the same way a home builder would.

Because you handle the same types of cases all the time, the process is familiar to you, but you need to paint that picture for the client.

The goal of a consultation is for the potential client to feel informed, to know that you can solve the problem that he or she has, and to understand the value of what you are offering. This is where the sales presentation comes in.

a. Handouts

You can create your sales presentation using handouts, printed quote sheets, and document lists that you will provide to clients in a branded folder.

No matter what, people who come to your office should always leave with something that is printed out and has your letterhead on it.

You should provide the client with a handout that gives a step-by-step breakdown of the legal process, one that focuses on large case milestones that are important to them.

This needs to be a simple guide to the legal case.

In a family case, for example, it could be something like:

1. File for divorce.
2. File the parenting plan.
3. Go to court to get a temporary judge's order about child custody.
4. Take the parenting class.
5. Finalize divorce in court.

In between these important steps, you have to file motions for temporary orders, motions to finalize the divorce, and more. However, those are not relevant to the client, so they should not be included on the list.

A very simple checklist is best—something that says, step 1, step 2, etc. I find bullet points work well, too, to keep things simple, organized, and easy to understand.

Not only will this help the client understand the process better, a handout will keep you on track when you are doing your value-based quoting and speaking to the client about the case. It will help ensure that you are telling only the most important information to the client, not all the information available.

As an added benefit, when you are training new staff members who have never worked in your area of practice, they can use the checklist to understand the entire process and be able to answer the "what comes next" question that they will inevitably get from clients.[2]

b. Printed quote sheets

No one should ever leave your consultation without taking away a written quote. Telling a potential client a quote without writing it down leads to confusion. Imagine—they are overwhelmed, scared, and they have exposed their problem to someone for the first time. They are getting information about their legal case for the first time. Then on top of it all, they are trying to remember the legal fee.

You can see why writing it down is helpful. On your quote sheet, you should write:

- The name of the legal process that you are offering

- The legal fee

- The filing fees

- Any additional fees and costs

- A list of what your legal fee includes

---

[2] You will find sample checklists in Step 5, "Streamlining Your Law Firm."

It is very important to have all these elements on your quote sheet; that way, it is a reference for both you and your client in the future. Ideally, all this will be enumerated in your contract as well, but this is still an important starting point for the lawyer/client relationship. Start with transparent communication about money. Without transparency and full understanding, it can cause dissatisfaction and disputes between both parties in the future.

If you do the same type of cases on a regular basis, create quote sheets for each case type. You can make folders by case type in advance, using the handout, the quote sheet, and the document list that I'll discuss next. This will help you stick to your pricing—since it is already pre-written and printed, you will be "forced" to stick with it.

c. Document lists

The final piece to your sales pitch is a written list of documents and information that you need from the client. One of the four questions that a potential client needs answered during a consultation is, "What do you need from me?" The document list answers that question.

A lot of lawyers hesitate when I tell them to give a document list at the consultation. They are afraid that the client will then take that list and go and do the case themselves. I felt the same way.

But my response now is:

> We can't control what someone will or won't do, so I don't want to spend my energy living in fear around it. If they take a document list and go and do their own case, it means that they were likely going to do that anyway.

I talk a lot about finding your ideal client and marketing to them in my book, *Be the CEO of Your Law Firm: Gain Control, Turn a Profit, and Reclaim Your Life.*[3] Once you know who your ideal client is

---

[3] Find *Be the CEO of Your Law Firm* on Amazon at *https://www.amazon.com/dp/1732082502.*

and how to find that person, it is very unlikely that you will attract someone to your office who wants to do a case on his or her own—instead, they will be expecting to work with you.

Extreme efficiency is a goal of my law firm. Giving a potential client a document list means that when he or she comes to sign up, that person is 100 percent ready to go on the case. When you don't give a document list until the client signs up, you end up spending months chasing the client down to get the documents that you need. You become a client babysitter. It is extremely ineffective for all parties involved. It drains your firm's resources. The client is unhappy because it causes delays in the case.

On the document list, I also include instructions on how to start the case, which makes it easy for the client to understand "what's next."

It says:

How to Get Started with the Case

- Call my office to schedule a 2-hour appointment.

- Bring the payment and any documents from the list.

- We will sign a contract and get working on the case the same day.

d. Branded folders

Your handouts, quote sheet, and document list should be assembled in a branded folder. At first, I simply used a two-pocket folder with a mailing label with my firm name, address, and phone number on the front, and my business card and business manager's business card inside. It's a great way to provide a branded look in an inexpensive way.

My client folders are now printed professionally using *Vistaprint*, which offers quality printing with reasonable prices. We use colored folders to distinguish the different cases and I have them in my drawer at my desk. When I do the consultation and determine that the potential client is eligible for a certain form of relief, I pull out the appropriate folder and start my sales presentation.

First, I walk the client through the handout that has the case overview. Next, I go through the quote sheet. Finally, I end with the document list and how to get started on the case.

The sales presentation folder helps keep me "on script." It helps me stick with the most important points of the case instead of getting stuck in over-explaining.

Once you put together your sales presentation and start using it with clients, you will find the best wording for everything that you want to convey to the client.

My clients eventually use their folders to keep themselves and their documents organized. For example, clients come to my office with all their documents in the folder, in the order that is listed on the document list.

Another side benefit that some lawyers have shared with me is that their clients are giving them free advertising while carrying around their folders. One lawyer, who works with athletes, said that while her clients were carrying around the folder in the locker room, another guy saw it, said he needed a lawyer, and he was able to get all of her contact information right there from the folder. I love that!

5. A good sales technique provides a strong finish

If someone doesn't retain you on the spot, how do you follow up after the consultation? Do you send a letter? Do you send an email? Do you give the person a call?

One thing that is very easy to do is sending a thank-you note to every person who comes to your office for a consultation. On Vistaprint, you can order "Thank You"postcards that have your logo and firm information.

On the back, you can write a short note such as:

> "It was a pleasure meeting you today! I look forward to helping you with your case. Sincerely, _____."

We follow up with a phone call within a week; and if the person hasn't retained our firm in 30–45 days, I or someone in my office calls to follow up with that person to answer any questions he or she might have or see if there is any additional information the person might need in order to make a decision.

Consider the "after-the-consultation period" the time when you must woo the client. You need to show that person how important his or her case is to you and that you are willing to go the extra mile.

Incorporating Value-Based Quoting into Your Consultations

Selling is all about leading with the *value* of your services.

Value-based quoting is where you focus on the value of what you are providing—from the legal remedies that you are providing to the service that your law firm offers.

Let me tell you a secret: People do not walk away from a contract because of price. Almost never. They walk away from a contract because they do not understand the value they will receive from signing a contract with you.

Through value-based quoting, you are going to focus on communicating with the client all of the value that your services provide. This can be done by focusing on what it is that your client wants or needs.

Value-based quoting goes way beyond just sales techniques—it dives deep into helping you value your work and then shows you how to communicate that value to your clients.

The interesting thing about lawyers is that we have to first convince ourselves of the value that we provide! In order to do value-based quoting, you have to dig deep within yourself. This is because we devalue what it is we do.

How many times have you charged very little to do a legal task because it is easy for you to do? Let's say it's something that takes you 10–15 minutes to complete. Do you charge for it?

The answer should be a resounding "yes!" Because it only takes 15 minutes for you to do it means that you are an expert at doing that thing. And that has immense value.

For example, in my immigration law firm, preparing a work permit renewal is very easy—quick work even. A lot of immigration lawyers will do it for free or cheap because it is so quick and easy.

But this is a *huge* deal. That work permit, which takes only minutes to renew, allows a client to have job security. It allows him or her to have a driver's license. It allows the client to provide for his or her family, further his or her career, and find personal and professional success.

Wouldn't you agree that there's immense value in that?

Additionally, it took time to learn how to handle the work that goes into getting a work permit. For example, a wills and trusts attorney couldn't necessarily complete a work permit application for a client, while an immigration attorney wouldn't necessarily know how to advise a client on the probate process.

Our knowledge and experience come from on-the-job training coupled with years of formal education.

Wouldn't you agree that there's value in that as well?

Once we're able to see the value in ourselves, we can express it to our clients. That's what value-based quoting is all about.

Lesson Learned: Know your value

I used to charge $3,500 for a case type, and it was a case type that I hated. It was tedious. It was draining. The clients were almost always high maintenance. Then I found that another attorney whose practice was well-known for handling this type of case was charging more than four times as much. While I had no doubt that this attorney was an expert in this particular case type, I found myself saying, "She's no better than I am, so who does she think she is to charge so much?"

That's when reality set in. My negativity toward her was all a reflection of a judgment of myself. I was severely undervaluing myself, my experience, and my practice. Why wasn't I charging fees that reflected my worth and my value to my clients?

Case types that I considered easy were only easy because I possessed the experience and skills to make them seem easy. And I had the client success stories to back it up.

When it came to that other lawyer's pricing, I realized she was basing her pricing on the value of her work. She knew what to build into her price (the complexity of the case, the high-maintenance client, the daily administrative tasks, and the unpredictable things) to arrive at a price that accurately reflected her knowledge, ability, skill, expertise, and experience.

I knew she wasn't better than I am, but there was a huge difference between us. She knew her value and how to communicate that clearly to her clients. I didn't.

1. The entire consultation, or sales presentation, needs to focus on value

Because being a lawyer is the only thing that I know how to do, it is very easy for me to take my knowledge and experience for granted. Performing legal work is second nature for me. It's almost like breathing. And there are certain cases I could probably do in my sleep. But the ease of which I might perform certain tasks is no less valuable simply because they are easy; every time I use my expertise, I am creating something of value.

Value-based quoting requires that you pull the value out of what you are doing. Let's say that you file a case for a client, something you do every day. But this experience is life-changing for the client. This is the first step toward his or her new life, new chapter, or next level of his or her success. This is no big deal to you, but it's huge to your client.

When you downplay your value, both you and the client suffer. But it can be hard to find the right words, and that is where the concept of value-based quoting comes in.

For example, I was working with an attorney on how to do a flat fee for a contested divorce. There are a lot of contingencies that she wanted to take into consideration; we finally landed on $15,000 as a flat fee for the case.

Then we practiced her approach to the client:

> I know that this is a difficult time for you. You have enough chaos in your life right now. I want you to be sure that if you need me, you can reach out to me without worrying about whether the phone call will cost you money. You need to be able to plan for the costs of having a lawyer.
>
> A lot of lawyers charge by the hour, and the last thing you need to be worried about is how much I'm going to bill you every month.
>
> That is why I do things a little differently. I charge a flat fee that includes everything. That means filing fees, court visits, phone calls, meetings, depositions, mediation, and more. You will never pay another cent to this firm, and you will know you are protected by us. You will know we have your back.
>
> Our fee is $15,000 and we will fight hard to protect your interest and help guide you through this difficult time. You can do a down payment of $5,000, which is the typical retainer fee that any lawyer would request. Then, we can either do monthly payments for the balance or two lump payments after that.
>
> You will know that we are here for you for anything and everything, regardless of what may happen in your case.

Do you see how that sells the value? Don't make the fee the focus. Place the focus on what you can offer the client.

You offer so much value to your clients. Spend the consultation focusing on that value, reassuring the client, and answering these questions:

1. Can you help me?
2. How long will it take?
3. How much will it cost?
4. What do you need from me?

2. Talk to your clients with honesty and empathy

A few years ago, a family member of mine was diagnosed with cancer. He was a young guy, in his 20s, and his cancer was stage 4 and aggressive. It was a difficult time for everyone involved. But every time we would meet with his doctor, the doctor would tell him, "I want you to live. You deserve a long life." Or things like, "I will never stop fighting for you. I want you to be with your family. I want you to be able to have children."

No matter how grim the situation, those words were exactly what everyone wanted and needed to hear at the time. I remember thinking that I wanted to somehow implement this display of empathy in my practice. I had always felt that way about my clients but I never expressed it.

Now, I make a point of incorporating empathy when talking to clients. "I want you to win this. I will never stop fighting for you."

Clients want you to understand their plight, empathize with them, and vow to do everything you can to help them. And if you are able to accomplish this in a genuine way, then the fee discussion becomes easy.

This approach can work for family lawyers, immigration lawyers, even estate-planning lawyers. For example, an estate-planning lawyer could say:

> I want to make sure that your will is rock-solid because I want to ensure that you can provide for your family the way that you envision.

By talking to your clients with honesty and empathy, it shows that you are so much more than a high price tag. Your value will shine through and you will feel more confident with setting your fees.

3. Focus on the benefits you provide to the client

When you give a value-based quote, the entire presentation is focused around the benefits to the client. Note that this is entirely different from how most lawyers do it. Most lawyers will spend too much time talking about the legal process and legal theories.

This is not what the client wants to know! The client wants to know what benefit he or she will receive from the process.

Let's say you do personal injury law and you are quoting a client on your representation.

Here's how to do it wrong:

> Okay, great, we need to file a claim for your accident and try to talk to the insurance company. Then I have to talk to the medical companies to see if they can put litigation holds on all of your medical bills. We have to get everything together and start to negotiate with the insurance companies, which can be difficult. So if that doesn't work then what we have to do is file a complaint in court.
>
> This case is on contingency, which means that I only get a portion of whatever you get paid, which is 33% plus costs.

I don't do personal injury, so I am fudging it, but you get the idea.

Here's how to do it right with value-based quoting:

> I know you have been through a lot, and I am going to help you through this process. My goal is to get you the best settlement that I can. I know you are struggling right now with medical bills, and I can help with that. I'll make sure that you don't have to pay the bills right now and protect you from going to collections.
>
> The way that my fee works is that our firm is paid 33% of whatever amount we are able to obtain for you. While the process is going on, you do not pay my office anything. There will be some costs associated with your representation, which will also be paid at the end.
>
> My goal is to get you an amount of money that will compensate you for all that you have suffered and that will provide for you in the future. First, I will negotiate with the insurance companies and I will update you along the way about the progress. It is unlikely that we will have to go to court, but if that comes up in the future, then that's something we can talk about when it happens.

Do you see the difference?

In both situations, you inform the client of the process. But in the second situation, you are explaining the value that you are going to give to the client. For example, in the first situation, I said, "litigation holds on your medical bills." Yes, maybe the client will understand that. But that doesn't address your client's pain points. Your client is likely overwhelmed by the bills piling up and doesn't know what to do because he's likely out of work and/or working decreased hours. The words "litigation hold" don't really address this.

When you instead say, "I'll make sure you don't have to pay the bills right now and protect you from going to collections," you are telling the client the value that you will provide instead of explaining how you are going to do it. Again, the clients don't care about the "how" (*i.e.*, litigation hold)— they just want to know what you are going to accomplish for them.

Value-based quoting actually makes you value your own work more. When you start to see everything that you do from the value that it brings, it makes you more comfortable with your fees. It makes you evaluate all that you do for clients, see it from their perspective, and put into words that your clients can understand and appreciate. Value-based quoting most likely will help you increase your prices.

There is huge value in the way that we handle communication with our clients, and we should not simply sit back and hope that they realize it. We must tell them.

There are so many benefits to value-based quoting. Let's go through a few of them:

1. Your consultations will run more smoothly.
2. Your price quote is sandwiched in the middle of your presentation. This means that you don't have to dread it so much that you push it to the end. You talk about the value, then you talk about the price, then you talk about more value and what's needed to get started.
3. You will instantly increase client satisfaction.
4. Your number of contracts will increase.
5. You set boundaries and expectations from the beginning.

Value-based quoting applies to booking consultations as well.

Here's how to do it wrong:

> When people call to schedule a consultation, you say, "A consultation is $150." They are left with nothing more than the price. Instead, sandwich the price between value-based information.

Here's how to do it right.

When someone asks, "How much is a consultation?" Your answer should be:

> A consultation is scheduled for 1 hour in our office in _____, and is $150. During that time, you will meet one-on-one with the attorney and ask her all of the questions you have, and she will tell you your legal options.

Do you see the difference?

A lot of people want to know the price of a consultation, but they likely don't know what it entails. Many people who are calling your office have never worked with a lawyer before. They don't know what to expect. All that they know to ask for is the price. By responding with value-based quoting, you will set their expectations and also help them see why the consultation price is worth the investment.

Take your three main case types and experiment with your wording on how to do a value-based quote. As you begin to look at the value that you give to your clients, I invite you to give your quote a hard look. Make sure it reflects all the work that you do and covers every piece of the client experience.

Overcoming Objections

One of the biggest struggles we have with sticking with our pricing is when we hear someone make what we perceive to be an objection.

For example, if we say that our fee is $10,000 and the person says, "Wow, $10,000. That's a lot. Can't you give a discount or something?"

We usually will take that as an objection. We feel they are rejecting it. But it's not an objection, really. It's a complaint.

They are complaining about the price being too high in the same way you complain that it's hot out when it's 100 degrees. It's nothing different.

When someone is putting forth a complaint, the best way to handle it is to acknowledge it and move forward.

In the example above, many lawyers start feeling the pressure. They start thinking they should lower the price. They start second-guessing their quote. They start worrying that they are going to lose the deal. They start thinking things like, "Oh, I feel bad they probably can't afford it," or "I am probably asking for too much," or one that women in particular think, "Maybe I am being greedy with my fee."

But if you've implemented value-based quoting, you know that your quote reflects your value. You know the great work and great results that you will bring to a client. So you know, then, that the solution is not to cut your price.

Instead, the *first* thing you do when someone complains is you agree.

> I agree with you that it is a lot of money.

That's it. There's no need to argue that point.

Second, you go into your value-based presentation.

> I agree with you that it is a lot of money, though it is an investment into your future. You have a problem right now that needs a solution. I am going to help you solve it.

This is a general statement because you can tailor this to whatever area of law you practice.

For example, an estate-planning attorney might say:

> I agree with you, it is a lot of money. However, I want you and your family to be protected in the event of one of your deaths. Establishing these wills and specialized trusts are going to do just that.

What if the person responds:

Well, I see a need for it, it's not that I don't, it's just that it's a lot of money.

Third, you create urgency.

In order for people to make a decision, they have to feel there is an urgent reason to do so. When people ponder a decision, studies show they start to compare two dissimilar things—and they will diminish the one they want. For example, they will compare $10,000 of legal fees to new furniture for the living room.

This is why you must create urgency. Some lawyers feel uncomfortable with the idea of creating urgency; they feel "slimy" or "car salesman-like," but it isn't slimy or salesy to tell the truth about a situation.

Let's take the situation above where we are talking about $10,000 for wills and trusts for a family. As the lawyer, you know all the ways that going unprotected could completely ruin someone's life. You know the ways that someone's estate could unravel and children could go unprotected, especially in situations of a blended family where there are complex custody issues. You know all the things that can go wrong if the client does not invest in these legal protections for his or her family.

However, the client does not know. This is why you need to tell him or her. And you need to tell that person in the strongest way possible so that he or she can truly understand what not investing in your services will mean to his or her family and their lives.

Again, you don't want to over-explain. Keep it concise.

> I understand where you are coming from, but I am not exaggerating here when I say that this is a situation of life and death. Unfortunately, unexpected things happen—car accidents, cancer, and more. The last thing that I would want to happen is for your daughter to not get any of the estate that you have worked hard to create for her. As it stands right now, without any protection, she will be left out completely. This means that her basic needs can go unaddressed completely. If you were to pass away tomorrow, what would she be left with? She is only 5 years old, and since your wife would not have legal custody of her since she is the stepparent, there would be no requirement that any of the money from your es-

tate goes to care for her. And this is just the beginning. That's why this is an investment into your family and your legacy. You want to be sure that your wife and all of your children are cared for.

Maybe in this situation, there would be an objection such as:

> Well my wife loves her and would care for her.

Your response could be something like:

> I have no doubt that she would and that she loves your daughter. However, if your wife were to remarry or pass away, then the entire estate would pass to her husband. By setting up a trust now, the moment that you pass away, all of your assets would be divided automatically the way that you would want—you would ensure that no matter what happens in the future, every child would be given his or her fair share, in addition to your wife.

Note that you don't need to give myriad case anecdotes. Instead, you could just state the facts as they apply to this particular case. If you don't do _____, then _____. That's it.

Let me give you an example from my own practice. I am an immigration attorney. If a person in my jurisdiction is caught by immigration officials and he has been convicted of a DUI in the past, that person will be brought to immigration jail and he will not receive a bond. And people with DUIs are specifically targeted by immigration for detention.

So if a person comes to my office and has a past DUI conviction, I say something like this:

> "Listen, I know that this is a lot of money and a big investment. However, if you do not do something now to protect yourself, then there is a very high risk that you will be targeted by immigration, arrested, and detained. If you are brought to immigration jail, I want to be very clear with you that you will NOT be able to get out on bond. That means that you will be detained for months, or maybe even more than a year, if you are picked up. This is why you need to act now."

Do you see the urgency that I have created? It's 100 percent true.

It is a fact that this person is at very high risk if he or she doesn't do something. The inner workings of the immigration system likely aren't something that this person knows about, but I do—so I express it in a way that creates urgency in the person's mind.

I don't know if immigration will come looking for that person to-morrow, just like an estate-planning attorney doesn't know if his or her client will pass away the next day, but we do know that these things happen. If the client doesn't hire you before one of these un-fortunate events occurs, then it will be very problematic for him or her.

Also, creating urgency helps alleviate the fear that the client will walk away. Unlike what we think, clients don't normally walk away because of price. They walk away because we have failed to show them how important and valuable our services are. Urgency can be considered the same as importance.

Whenever clients object—on price or anything else—go through the three steps:

- Step 1: Agree—don't challenge them. Agree with their com-plaint.

- Step 2: Give value-based information. Make sure to highlight the value that you are bringing to them.

- Step 3: Create urgency. Show them how important it is to get started on their legal case right now.

Creative Upselling

Traditionally in sales, upselling refers to getting a client to buy a more expensive product. For example, if a person enters a car dealer-ship wanting a $20,000 car, then you upsell him to a $30,000 car, which better suits his needs.

Within the law profession, there really isn't a way to do a traditional "upsell." You quote and deliver the legal services that apply to the client. That's it.

Moreover, once a case concludes, there is usually nothing more that the client needs from you. This is why it is hard to build ongoing value in a legal business—most clients come for one or two transactions—and that is all they need.

But I want to challenge you to get creative. I want you to take a look at what you do to see if there is something more that you can offer outside of your current legal services in order to serve your clients.

There are some things that clients always ask you about or ask you to do that are outside of your contract, right? There are things that could benefit them in some way, but either you don't do it or don't know how to do it. Right now, I want you to think about those things.

But do not be tempted to perform these extra services for free; everything that goes beyond the scope of your contract can and should be charged for. Our businesses exist to make money and to provide clients a service that we know will serve them and make their lives better in some way.

As you develop services to upsell, I want you to remain committed to selling these services completely separate from your primary legal fee. I want you to be sure that these are separate and distinct from the main work that you are contracted to perform.

Consider offering certain products related to your representation, such as:

- Downloadable handbooks or eBooks

- Webinars

- Checklists and fillable forms

- Infographics and charts

- A monthly subscription service for follow-up questions

- On-demand legal service packages

- Non-legal ancillary services (*i.e.*, helping people apply for the Global Entry program after they obtain legal residency)

Consider this: A webinar can be sold numerous times to numerous people, and you would be reaching those who need it the most. Even potential clients can purchase access to the webinar to receive great information from you.

Webinars are an opportunity to sell your services by focusing on the benefits of your services and the urgency of the situation as discussed above under "Overcoming Objections" and "Incorporating Value-Based Quoting into Your Consultations."

The hardest part is trying to figure out what your upsell is going to be. Let's walk through some scenarios:

A family law scenario:

> After a case is closed, a family law attorney could offer to update the client's will or advance directive. Updating a will or advance directive to reflect the changes in the client's marital status could be easily overlooked by the client, but it is still very important. Of course, you would have to learn how to do it, but it could be a great additional service.

> Or

> A family law attorney could start a monthly subscription service for handling questions that occur after the case has been resolved. For example, child custody questions can arise after the divorce is final.

A trademark law scenario:

> A trademark attorney is likely working with people who are building brands and/or new businesses. She could have a business startup package that gives important information about building a business—like "Starting a Business 101."

An employment law scenario:

> An employment law attorney could offer an "on call" monthly package where she would be available for a certain number

of hours each month for employment questions after her initial work is finished. She could also create and sell a Human Resources handbook or a Human Resources package that would help prevent employment issues in the future.

These are just a few ideas to get you started thinking about additional products and services that you can provide based on your law practice. Finding ways to continue the attorney/client relationship is part of the upsell and the services you offer can continue to provide a worthy service to the client.

Once you know what your "upsell" will be, be mindful of how you communicate your new product or service to your client to avoid confusion and objections.

1. Communicate the new service in a positive way

The first step is to explain your upsell very concisely. Imagine being your client hearing from his lawyer that he can receive an additional service, but it comes with an additional cost. This is something that he didn't know about from the beginning, so he isn't expecting it.

It isn't something that would impact the outcome of his case, but if you fail to communicate this correctly, the client will think there is a case-related issue that you failed to inform him of.

2. Place yourself in your client's shoes

The second step is to think of all the objections the client might have. Money definitely will be the first one. Distrust of the process or system could be another. You have to be ready with your value-based presentation to combat the fears and the objections.

You will likely encounter "objections" (which we know are just complaints), such as:

- "I already paid you so much money, so why would I pay you more?"

- "Why isn't that included in my price? I thought I was paying you to take care of everything."

- "Honestly, I've spent enough on my case. I don't want to spend another cent."

- "I want results from my case before I would spend anything more on you."

You have to be prepared for these objections, and you have to stay strong in the face of them.

Here are some examples of what your response could be:

- "I can see why you would think that, but this is actually not related to the legal work in your case. Instead, this is something that is purely a benefit for you and is completely outside of your legal case."

- "I understand. This is completely different from your legal case, and it is a special opportunity that I wanted to bring directly to you."

- "I get it. I can see how it would seem like this would be part of my legal representation; however, it is separate and distinct from the case work that I am doing for you."

Developing products and services to upsell to your clients takes time and planning. You want to ensure that anything you offer provides additional value above and beyond the services you are currently providing to your clients.

Take the time to dissect your practice to see what more you can do to help your clients and how best to present those add-ons.

What You Need to KNOW:

☐ How to articulate the value that you provide to your clients

☐ The questions clients need answered

☐ All the elements that comprise your flat fee in order to develop a quote sheet

☐ What products or services that are related to your representation, which you can offer to clients in addition to your representation

What You Need to DO:

☐ Incorporate sales techniques into your consultation by focusing on the value you provide to your clients

☐ Quote your pricing without feeling uneasy

☐ Focus your responses on the questions clients need answered

☐ Be prepared to overcome objections

☐ Incorporate visuals to help explain a complicated process

☐ Present additional services to keep the client relationship going

IT'S ALL ABOUT THE CLIENT

"You never call except when you want money."

Our clients are the heartbeat of our law firms. Without clients, our firms would not exist. But we also find ourselves complaining about our clients. How many lawyers groups on Facebook are filled with people complaining about their clients? Too many to count.

Lawyers especially vent about those clients who have expressed dissatisfaction with their services, or have complained about how long things are taking, or have shared their frustration about never hearing from the lawyer.

What's behind all this? These complaints can be attributed to a lack of meaningful, regular communication between the lawyer and his or her clients. Communicating with clients can be stressful, especially when the case has taken an unexpected turn, or when things are delayed for reasons outside of your control, or when the case hasn't been submitted yet for one reason or another (waiting on documents, a possible law change, or some other emergency having taken precedence).

The secret to helping de-stress and empower client relationships is through over-communication.

Over-communication is key to making your client relationships thrive. It increases client satisfaction. It allows clients to have a more active role in their cases and lessens their anxiety.

When I was interviewed on the *"Gen Why Lawyer"*[1] podcast, we discussed an interesting phenomenon about client communication.

When a client is the one who initiates communication with you and your office, it is stressful. We feel defensive. Oftentimes, we don't even want to take the call. Even if the client just wants a quick update on the case, we somehow feel like we're under attack. We imagine the client accusing us of not having done something or not having done enough. Essentially, no matter what the client says, we feel stressed out by it, even if it results in a simple cordial, quick call.

But when we initiate communication with clients, we have the opposite reaction. Even if it's just a call, email, or text to say that all is going well in the case and there is no update, the conversation goes surprisingly well, and we remain upbeat, and stress-free. Usually, clients are happy to hear from us. They even express appreciation for the contact.

Imagine if regular client contact were a policy in your law firm. Imagine if clients were hearing from you all the time without ever having to contact you first. Imagine avoiding those uncomfortable situations when an annoyed client says, "You never call except when you want money." (I've heard that one many times, unfortunately.)

"Step 4: It's All About the Client" focuses on ways to improve communication with your clients and how to handle situations brought on by a lack of communication. It discusses the pitfalls of over-explaining concepts in favor of keeping things simple; it gets you to focus on answering the primary questions that all clients have; it shows you how to handle awkward moments caused by miscommunication; it helps you face disgruntled clients; and it shows you how to deliver news your clients might not want to hear.

---

[1] Gen Why Lawyer: "Implementing great systems and building a 7-figure practice with Ally Lozano," *http://www.genylawyer.com/158-2/*.

We will cover:

1. Communicating with Clients in a Way They Understand;
2. Automating Your Consultation with Customer Service in Mind;
3. Handling Client Misunderstandings with Empathy;
4. Nurturing Plus Over-communication: The Building Blocks of a Solid Attorney/Client Relationship; and
5. Communicating Bad News to Your Clients.

Communicating with Clients in a Way They Understand

Clients can be the most frustrating part of the job sometimes. They can be needy, overbearing, and demanding. However, part of the problem is that they don't know how to work with lawyers. Most clients have never worked with a lawyer before. They don't know what to expect or how to interact with us.

The only way they can learn how to have a productive lawyer/client relationship is if we teach them how best to work with a lawyer.

This problem recently came up in my practice because I have a client who is illiterate and has never been to school a day in her life. When my assistant called the client to request biographical information as part of our client intake, I received an angry call from the client. She said that she hired an attorney so that she wouldn't have to do anything, and if we were going to ask her questions then she did not understand why she had to pay an attorney.

My first reaction was annoyance. People should understand that, as attorneys, we are not magicians, nor are we clairvoyant. I would not magically know the names of my client's siblings and her children's dates of birth.

Then I took a moment to think of it from her perspective. She is uneducated. She doesn't even know how to write her name. She mistakenly believed that her attorney would not need her involvement. I realized that she does not understand what an attorney does and what I can and cannot do without her. I then took the opportunity to set her expectations appropriately and help her understand the limitations I have as her representative. She was extremely happy about it, and our relationship was excellent from that point on.

Here are a few ways to help teach your clients how to have a successful working relationship with you as their attorney:

1. Talk to clients in a way they understand

As lawyers, we over-explain things. We give way too much information. Clients need the basics: Can you help me, yes or no? When will it be done? How much does it cost? That's all they really want to know. Most of the time, they don't care about the strategy. They don't care how you get there.

Don't get into the legal strategies and theories. Those are only exciting for us lawyers. To the client, it isn't fun and it doesn't help—it's confusing. Clients only want to know the benefits that will come to them through the case. Over-explaining simply leads to confusion. If clients want to know more about legal strategies, then mention it only if asked; but even then, keep it very simple and concise.

2. Get to the point.

Really. Get to the point.

Do not explain the nuances. Do not discuss every contingency and slight possibility. There's no need.

When I emailed my IP attorney about something I wanted to have trademarked, she wrote back:

> "Let's do it. It may not work because they may not accept it—depending on what they say, we can respond in different ways. We'll just go for it, try our best, and make a plan from there."

And then she told me the price. Perfect. That's all I needed to know.

I didn't need to know the legal reasons why it could be denied. I didn't need to know the possible legal arguments. I didn't actually care. Anything that she said at that point would be speculative. All I needed to know is that no matter what happened, she would come up with a plan. I can assure you, it was the best email I've ever received from a lawyer.

Speak like this to your clients. It respects them and their needs more, not less, by talking to them in a way they can understand without over-explaining every little thing.

3. Set expectations from the beginning

When the client signs up, describe to the client the amount of contact he or she can expect to have with you. For example, you can explain that the legal assistant and legal secretary will be able to answer the majority of questions he or she may have and that a lot of their contact will be with them.

If you do not handle the sign-up yourself, be sure to tell your clients this in the consultation so that they understand they will not meet with you directly when they sign up.

4. Explain your team approach in the contract

In your contract, it is a good idea to include language such as, "Any and all members of [Law Firm], and anyone hired therein, may work on your case." This helps cover any contract attorneys or paralegals you might hire, including staff hired on a contract basis. This also gives an opportunity for you to explain to the client that your firm works as a team and that you will not be the only person who communicates with him or her about the case.

5. Use visual handouts

Legal cases are confusing. Many lawyers speak in legalese without even intending to do so, which makes it even more confusing for the client. Also, most clients are going through some sort of difficult, overwhelming, or scary experience, which is why they need a lawyer's help. In that emotional/mental state, it is even harder to understand the information being explained by the attorney. This is when visual handouts help the most.

For example, a checklist that lays out every step of the case that can be checked off as each step is completed can be very helpful for a client. A detailed letter to the client giving an overview of the entire case, but in a succinct bullet-pointed and/or numbered format, is helpful as well.

Of course, as the lawyer, it is easy to "see" the process. You know what is next. You know where you are going. But the client has never navigated the path before and he or she needs a map.

If you make that map for the client, the client will be better equipped to collaborate with you. This can make for a stronger case, and it will also cut down on the questions and the "neediness" that some of us experience from clients.

Clients won't ask you the same questions over and over because your materials will explain it all to them.

I have used the services of several lawyers and I have never had one provide me with written materials with an overview of the case. Most of the legal processes in which I have been involved were foreign and confusing to me—and I *am* a lawyer! I wish my lawyers would have done this for me.

6. Keep it simple[2]

Assure your client that his or her problem can be handled. Address his or her most pressing questions:

- Can you help me?

- What do you need from me?

- How much will it cost?

- Tell me what to do and I'll do it. Then let me know the end result.

Your response should be simple:

- This is what we can do.

- This is what we can't do.

- This is what I will do.

- This is what I need from you.

- Let's get started.

- You make the down payment, and I get to work.

---

[2] To learn more about how to address the most pressing client questions, see "Step 3: Conquering Sales with Confidence and Authenticity" in the section on Incorporating a Sales Presentation into Your Consultation Without Sounding Salesy.

Automating Your Consultation with Customer Service in Mind[3]

The consultation is arguably the most important client interaction that you will have. It sets the tone for your firm and your attorney/client relationship. As the adage says, "You never get a second chance at a first impression." That's why you need to create an experience for your potential client that is unique and unforgettable.

1. Empathize with your client's situation

It is important to keep in mind that at the time of the consultation, your client is likely scared and stressed. Let's face it, most of the time, people come to an attorney when things are not going well in their lives.

This may be the first time your potential client has ever spoken with an attorney before. Maybe this person had to work up the nerve to call and schedule a consultation, attend the consultation, and then open up to a stranger about an uncomfortable, unhappy, and sometimes embarrassing situation or experience.

Keeping this in mind allows you to create an experience that honors your client and his or her emotions as your client navigates a difficult time in his or her life.

At my firm, we have created a "multi-layered" consultation where customer service is the focus at each step. Here's an overview of our process:

> The legal assistant brings out the Consultation Intake Sheet and greets the client and explains the intake sheet. She says the client's name no less than 3 times in the interaction.

---

[3] To learn how to take your consultation to the next level by incorporating a sales presentation, see "Step 3: Conquering Sales with Confidence and Authenticity" for the section on Incorporating a Sales Presentation into Your Consultation Without Sounding Salesy.

The legal assistant offers a beverage and even if the client says no, she makes hot chocolate anyway. ("People always love hot chocolate. It's delicious!"—Brenda, my former assistant, would say. I can't disagree with her on that one.)

The legal assistant brings the client back to her office to process the payment, prepare a receipt, and review the initial screening questions. During that time, she also puts the case in our case management system.

The legal assistant then brings the client to the offices of each person on the staff introducing him or her, explaining that person's role, and letting the client know how that person can serve him or her in the future.

The legal assistant brings the client to the lawyer's office for the consultation.

The lawyer introduces herself, explains confidentiality, and opens the consultation with the question, "So what brings you in today?"

The lawyer allows the client to speak without asking any questions except for clarification.

After the client has told his or her entire story, the lawyer begins asking questions to determine if the client has a case and the type of case.

The lawyer explains the case type and case overview. At the end, she asks, "Do you have any questions about anything I have explained? I know that it is very confusing, so please feel free to ask me anything."

The lawyer provides a written quote sheet that includes the price and case type.

The lawyer concludes the consultation by stating, "If you have any questions that you think of in the next few days, please do not hesitate to contact me or any member of our team. We are here to serve you."

The legal assistant returns to walk the client to the elevator, ensuring that the client does not have any further questions, and again reminds the client that he or she can call with any questions. During this interaction, the legal assistant will say the client's name at least 3 times.

At the same time, the lawyer writes a thank-you note to the client for coming in that says, "It was a pleasure to meet you. I look forward to serving you in your case." It is immediately placed in the mail so the client will have it 1–2 days after the consultation.

Within 24 to 48 hours of the consultation, a legal assistant calls the client to check in to see if there were any additional questions.

Our hope is that the client feels heard, understood, and that he or she has received information in a way that is meaningful.

2. Create scripts for client interaction[4]

Oftentimes, we are so caught up in lawyering that we forget what it's like to be the client sitting on the other side of the table. Take time to consider every single interaction that your clients have with your firm.

Think about how you want them to feel during those interactions. What do you want them to know? What should they understand about you, your firm, and the law at each interaction?

Walk through each of these steps with your staff. Create scripts for each interaction:

- Initial phone call

- Arrival to the office for the initial consultation

- Initial consultation

- Consultation follow-up

- Sign-up appointment

- Document signing for case submission

- Post-submission communication

---

[4] In chapter 4 of my book, *Be the CEO of Your Law Firm: Gain Control, Turn a Profit, and Reclaim Your Life*, I offer sample scripts for phone contact, consultation confirmations, and in-person greetings, which you can put to use in your law practice right away. Find it on Amazon at *https://www.amazon.com/dp/1732082502*.

- Communication of results (win, lose, or otherwise)

- Case closure

- Post-case closure

3. Document everything

Every client should receive a letter from you upon signing up that gives the overview of the steps in the case and a summary of the process. Each letter thereafter should explain the current step as well as provide the client another overview of the process. We oftentimes think clients will look into things themselves, but this is a bad assumption on our part.

I cover client communication and documentation in detail below under "Nurturing Plus Over-communication: The Building Blocks of a Solid Attorney/Client Relationship."

Handling Client Misunderstandings with Empathy

When it comes to client communication, there is something important that you need to remember: Clients are scared. They are nervous. Most clients have never worked with a lawyer before. Or maybe they have, but this is the first time they are working with a lawyer on this specific issue.

Clients aren't coming to you because things are going well in their lives. They are coming to you during a time of stress. They are coming to you at a time of uncertainty. They need your legal expertise and they need you to guide them through the legal process.

Even if they trust you as their lawyer, they are likely still getting "legal" opinions from other sources, such as friends and family, and my all-time favorite, Google. This type of advice will only result in more questions for them, more doubts, and even more fear.

They may bombard you with questions. Or they might get lost in their own thoughts and anxiety and accuse you of not doing enough.

If you're anything like me, I can get heated and defensive easily when I feel attacked. I especially get upset when clients say, "You aren't doing anything in my case; why am I paying you so much money to do nothing?"

Negative contact from a client typically stems from fear. When he or she is angry, belligerent, insulting, or just snappy, the client is only coming from a place of fear. When the client calls to ask you to confirm or dispel what a friend's neighbor's brother said, he or she is coming from a place of fear.

Let's first start from a place of understanding and acknowledgment of that fear.

When we change the perspective through which we view these conversations, it will help change the tone of the conversation. It will also de-escalate the situation.

1. Listen without interrupting

It's natural to react defensively when a client approaches you angrily. You'll want to interrupt, defend, correct, etc. However, resist! Do not interrupt; the client just wants to be heard. Let the client get it all out.

Sometimes, people need to get things off their chests; and then they feel better. Let your client express his or her frustrations and concerns. Listen without preparing a defense.

View it as the client simply venting to you about the problems he or she is having with you, your firm, and/or the case. Venting is a way to make our feelings and frustrations known to the other person. By accepting this, you can then react in a more solution-oriented manner.

No matter how well-run your law firm is, there always will be things that could be better. By acknowledging both your client's feelings and the ways you can improve, you can turn a heated discussion into a productive conversation.

Example:

> A client is upset because she feels you don't return her calls. But she has never left a message so you didn't even know she'd called.

Try this:

> I can hear that you are frustrated. I understand that you want to talk to me and you feel like I never call you back. I would be happy to call you back because I want to talk to you and your case is very important to me. On my end, I did not know that you called because I never received a message from you.

> So let's try this: When you call and you don't receive an answer, could you please leave a message? I promise that I will get back to you within 24 hours. Would that work for you?

Developing a solution that requires both of your cooperation can help move the relationship forward.

2. Acknowledge the problem

Acknowledge what the client has said and repeat it back to the client to show that you understand.

Example:

> "I hear that you are feeling frustrated because your case has been pending for six months and you do not yet have a work permit. Is that correct?"

If the client has something more to say, then let the client speak again without interrupting.

3. Use the phrase, "I understand"

Talk directly to the issues raised by the client without being defensive and use the phrase, "I understand."

Example:

> "I understand that this is very frustrating for you. It is frustrating for me, too. I want you to be able to provide for your family. The entire goal of our working together is [for you to have legal status in the United States] so that you can provide for your family and have a great life here."

If it involves a delay in the case, help the client understand the reason for the delay, but don't over-complicate it! Don't over-explain! Give a summary—break it down in the most fundamental way so that it is easy to understand. Get directly to the point. You don't need to give background or cite the law—just give a quick summary of what is going on.

4. Bring in a third party

If necessary, bring in a third party to help diffuse the situation. If the client is on the phone, I ask for permission to put him or her on speakerphone to facilitate a discussion with the business manager present.

If the client meets with me in person, I often will do the same because my manager can be more neutral and less emotionally charged. It doesn't bother him the way that it bothers me when someone accuses me of something.

Something important to remember is that when people are venting, they say things in the most extreme way possible even if they don't really mean it. Clients want reassurance. If you can't provide that in a calm and supportive way, bring in someone who can help.

5. Provide next steps

Draft a plan for next steps to help ensure satisfaction for both the client and you. Let the client know what, if anything, can and will be done in the case moving forward.

Example:

> "Usually, these are things that we do behind the scenes and we don't like to bother you with small details; however, if you would like to be informed each time we do this, I am happy to give you a call and let you know about it."

6. Follow up in writing

After the meeting is over, send an email or letter summarizing the meeting. Sum up the client's frustrations and the solutions that you came up with that require changes on both your parts.

7. Use firing as a last resort

Many lawyers want to fire a client when he or she gets angry. But if you take it as venting instead of an attack, you don't need to fire the client. You can rebuild trust and improve your communication. Good customer service skills can salvage many attorney-client relationships that are on the brink of demise.

If the problems are truly unfixable, then you might need to part ways. However, this should be the absolute last resort.

Conflicts with clients happen to the best of us. When clients get angry, frustrated, or confrontational, many of us panic. Oftentimes, we try to avoid the confrontation. However, an angry client is an opportunity for excellent customer service.

Nurturing Plus Overcommunication:
The Building Blocks of a Solid
Attorney/Client Relationship

You've done so much hard work to get the client to retain you.

The client has paid a price that reflects your value.

You've started on the work and will do your best to get great results for your client.

Now is the time to focus on client satisfaction because your responsibility to nurture the client has only just begun.

This is where we as lawyers falter. We don't nurture the client. We don't communicate with the client regularly. We don't call, email, or text the client. And we don't make our clients feel special.

We believe that our clients know we are busy doing the work. And when we have something to tell them, we will contact them, but not until then.

We rationalize our lack of communication by saying we don't want to bother our clients. Yet the number-one complaint that most clients have about their attorneys is the lack of communication.

The truth: Clients want to hear from you. They want to know that things are progressing in their cases, even if there is nothing to say. A quick email, text, or phone call that says, "Everything is pending and going well," goes a long way for a client.

Even if they don't ever express it, clients expect to hear from you regularly. They will never think of it as bothersome if you call them with updates on their cases. Ever.

Sending a scheduled update letter, calling the clients monthly, and sending season-themed postcards or greeting cards can be ways to let clients know you are working on their cases and that they are important to you.

The bottom line: Your client needs to feel like he or she is the most important person in your firm. This is what nurturing is.

The concepts of nurturing and over-communication are so simple and yet so daunting for many lawyers. And yet they are so important to our continued success.

Regular nurturing and over-communication help put your clients at ease. They help build trust during the course of the case and open the door to better communication overall.

Also, if clients know they will be hearing from you regularly, it lessens their need to reach out to you "just to check in" or to ask how the case is going. This will help put you at ease and will cause fewer interruptions.

Nurturing begins at the onset of your client relationship and remains ongoing. Over-communication plays a major role in the nurturing process.

Here are some ways you can nurture clients from the beginning:

1. The contract-signing appointment

How do you handle the contract-signing appointment? Who does it? What kind of experience do you want the client to have?

Make the client feel like his or her case is important and a high priority to you. Get started working on the case right away. Do the contract, payment, and then get right down to work in that same meeting. This meeting might last for up to three hours. During this meeting, schedule the date for the client to return—whether it is to sign documents, to bring in more documents, or to gather more information. Getting the next appointment on the calendar is imperative to keep the work on the case moving along. The date is ideally within one week, no more than two.

The power in scheduling the next appointment during your first one is to ensure that the client won't get "lost" or fall off the grid. The faster you can get the case completed and out the door, the more satisfied your client will be.

2. The post-contract signing period

How do you communicate with clients immediately after the contract is signed? What can you do to let the clients know how much you appreciate their business?

Send a small gift to every new client after sign-up. Send the gift after rather than offering the gift at sign-up so the client will feel remembered and important. It's a little something that says "we are thinking about you" a few days after the contract is signed and money has been exchanged.

Something as simple as a coffee mug with your company name and logo goes a long way to show your appreciation. Mugs could be about $10/piece, depending on how many you buy, but it is a small detail that will set you apart from other law firms.

Whether it's a coffee mug, a handwritten note, a thank-you card, or just a follow-up text, email, or phone call, you are doing something to thank someone for having confidence in you and your firm.

They have given you more than their money—they have given you their trust. Be sure to thank them for that.

3. During the case: Send general monthly emails

Each month, send an email indicating whether a case is pending, active, or if you are waiting on the client for something.

These emails cut down on the number of calls from clients regarding their case status. Clients feel informed. They are told that their cases are pending; that you are just waiting on a decision; that you are actively working on the case; or that you need them to contact your office.

4. During the case: Send case-specific monthly emails

How do you communicate with clients while you are waiting for a decision or for something to happen so you can take the next step?

In my immigration law practice, there are certain cases that will be pending based on processing times set by the government. We send a specific email by case type to each client about when the client's case was submitted and where the processing times are. It's a template letter; and while it does take time to update the letter each month, providing the letter is a fairly simple undertaking.

Communicating with your client during this time is critical. The phrase, "No news is good news," does not apply to clients. They assume, "No news is bad news."

Once a case is pending, this is when you should be increasing your customer service and over-communicating with clients. Ove-communication should be your goal.

To accomplish this, designate someone in your office to email these letters each month. In our firm, every case is labeled active, pending, or waiting on the client. We can run a report and see who falls into what category, which makes it very easy to know who should be notified about a pending case.

We also give updates by case type. We can easily process these by running different case reports using our case management system. This way, we know who to send the letters to each month.

Does this sound a bit time-consuming? Well, it is. But it is necessary. This will help your clients feel informed, cared about, and taken care of. As an added bonus, this will differentiate your firm from every other firm.

Nurturing your clients is all about serving your clients in the best way possible. You want your clients to know that you care about them. You want them to know that they are valued.

5. Call every client every month

It can be time-consuming to call all of your clients, but it should be your goal to call every client once a month. Clients often feel like they are bothering us if they call us, so take the first step and call them. It does not have to be the attorney who calls, though it is a good idea for the attorney to call the client at least once every two months or so.

The average call takes about 90 seconds. Yes, I have timed it.

Try to call every client each month just to check in and say that everything is going well in the case, or that you need something from them, etc.

Calling regularly puts your client's mind at ease. For example, let's say your client was injured in a car accident. He can't work, his bills are piling up, and he is getting collections calls constantly. He doesn't know how he's going to make ends meet.

More than likely, he is sitting at home thinking about how his case is going. "When will I hear from my lawyer?" "When will I have a settlement so I can pay my bills?" "When will I get a payout to cover my living expenses?"

Or maybe your client is going through a divorce. She is probably stressing about money, splitting property, and the well-being of her children.

A call from her attorney or someone in her attorney's office could help reassure her that everything is moving along smoothly.

6. If a client calls and needs to talk, schedule a formal phone meeting

This tip will transform your practice. Most lawyers, including me, are terrible at returning phone calls. A client would call my firm with a question that only a lawyer could answer, and my assistants would pass me the message telling me to return the call. I would then get too busy or simply forget to return the call (or I would procrastinate because I'm dreading having the conversation).

We came up with a life-changing solution. When a client has a question for me that no one else can answer, my assistant schedules the client for a 15-minute phone meeting with me. These calls typically take place between 9:00 am and 10:00 am before my usual consultations and client sign-ups.

This strategy makes the interaction more formal—and that helps me tremendously. Clients get their questions answered in a timely manner and they get direct contact with me. This is an easy way to make sure client communication and customer service are reflected as highly valued in our firm, and it goes a long way to making our clients feel nurtured.

Even though their case may be just another day at work for us, for our clients, it's their whole life. Commit to reaching out every month or every other month just to check in and give an update, even if the update is, "Your case is still pending."

Over-communication should be one of the tenets of your law firm, and it will change things for the better for your clients and for your team.

Lesson Learned: Clients don't think like lawyers

During the pendency of a case, I didn't think it was necessary to contact my clients just to say there was nothing happening. It was the type of case wherein the first step simply takes months. I wouldn't want to be bothered with such trivial stuff, so I figured my clients wouldn't want to be either.

In hindsight, however, I realize that I was thinking of myself as the client with the knowledge of a lawyer—which clients do not have. *My first mistake.*

Since I wasn't communicating with them, my clients began calling me. Almost every week. Instead of trying to ease their fears or communicate better, I told them that if they kept calling so often I would start charging them hourly for the calls.

In hindsight, I made this about me and not about my clients. I was annoyed, overwhelmed, and flustered, so I failed to see that my clients were just fearful and worried. *My second mistake.*

Finally, the first part of the case was approved. Yet to my chagrin, the immigration office had made a mistake in the processing, and now it would take months to fix it. I contacted my clients, and they demanded a meeting.

The couple was due to have a baby any day, and they were stressed about their case. They were frustrated. They were angry. But the wife wasn't angry about the mistake. She was angry about my lack of communication during the pendency of the case.

She said to me, "I know this is something that you do every day, but it's not something we do every day. This is our lives. This worries me when I wake up in the morning and when I go to bed at night. I think about it constantly. And then because I am so worried about it, I call you. And when I call you, you get mad and say I am calling too much. So, really, we don't know what to do."

I felt like I had failed in every way possible. I had achieved one result for my clients, yet I had failed in making my clients feel important. I had failed to put my clients at ease. I had failed to establish my clients' faith in me. I had failed to be their guide through this stressful time for them.

To make matters worse, soon after, something went wrong in the case. The husband accused me of doing it wrong. He even accused me of messing up the case in retaliation for their incessant calling. What went wrong had nothing to do with me, and I was insulted by his accusations.

In hindsight, I know that he was just venting about it. He was frustrated. I was frustrated. She was frustrated. *My third mistake.*

This case taught me a lesson. As lawyers, we want our clients to trust us and have faith in us. Establishing and maintaining open communication with clients are the building blocks for trust and faith. My clients had lost faith in me because I failed to lay that foundation and place their needs in high regard.

What my client said is true: As lawyers, we do this every day. We can easily see the processes from beginning to end. We know the expected outcome and we know how long it will take. We know everything is fine.

But clients don't know that. They constantly worry about it. They may even be obsessing over it. As a lawyer, it is easy to lose sight of this because you can see so clearly what will happen. You aren't emotionally involved in the same way as your client. We know there's an end in sight, but they don't know that.

7. The "case closed" appointment

What's your process for closing a case? Do you send a closing letter? Do you send a gift? Do you stay in touch after the case is over? How do you stay in touch?

Schedule a "case closed" meeting with your client to tie up any loose ends. Present him or her with a small token of your appreciation, something branded with your firm's name so that you stay top of mind.

8. Stay in contact with clients after the case has closed

Try to make working with a client more than just a transaction. You want to be the first person your client thinks of when a friend needs a lawyer. You want your clients to talk about what you did for them, how much attention you paid to them, how much you cared, and how important you made them feel.

- Send a quarterly postcard to all your existing and past clients, something to welcome each season.

- Email a monthly newsletter to keep your clients up to date on what's happening in your firm or important information that might impact them or someone they know. Use the opportunity to share success stories or to invite them to local events your firm is sponsoring.

- Hold a "Client Appreciation" happy hour at your firm and invite all current and past clients. Tell them to bring a friend.

These tips will help empower your client interaction and make the attorney/client relationship more fulfilling (and less frustrating) for you and your clients.

Communicating Bad News to Your Clients

Lawyers do not want to communicate bad news to their clients. But who does?

When people pay us to seek a certain outcome and we are unable to achieve that for them, we feel guilty—even if it isn't our fault. We don't want to disappoint our clients, so we delay telling them. We wallow in some form of self-blame.

These feelings and emotions paralyze us and make it hard to communicate with our clients.

Put an end to this behavior by coming up with a plan for communicating bad news or unfavorable results to your clients.

Here are some tips:

- As soon as you become aware of the situation, have your team schedule an in-person meeting with the client as soon as possible.

  Do not spend too much time agonizing over it and dragging your feet on finding a solution. When you have a firm policy in place that requires immediate action, you are forced to have the conversation—minus the agonizing, minus the inaction.

- In the time leading up to the appointment, assemble a plan of next steps. If there are no next steps, then there are no next steps. Embrace that as well.

- In the client meeting, speak directly and concisely.

Examples:

"I want to tell you that your case has been denied. I do not agree with the decision and I believe that this is something that has a chance to win on appeal."

Or

"We received the decision on your case and it was denied. Unfortunately, there are no other steps that we can take from here. Do you have any questions?"

- Allow the client to ask any questions he or she might have without interruption. The client might vent. The client might be upset. Allow the client to get it all out. Don't interrupt. Use the phrase, "I understand."

- Bring the conversation back to the next steps. If there is something that you can do, tell the client what it is, what the cost is, what you need from him or her to get started, and the deadline.

- If there is nothing you can do, provide the client with a letter explaining the denial and that there are no other options at this time.

- Continue client communication. Even if there is nothing more you can do, keep the client on your mailing list.

Bad news is best given directly and concisely. The clients want to know. They would rather know than not know. So give them what they want and need, even if it's hard for you. You haven't failed them just because you received bad news or didn't win their case.

The outcome isn't up to you. The final decision isn't in your hands. In most cases, you haven't made a mistake. You haven't failed to do something.

Don't make the mistake of making this about you. When we fail to properly communicate with clients, we are making it personal. But it isn't about us—at all. It's about the client.

Lesson Learned: Own up to your mistakes

To file paperwork by mail, we typically use FedEx for delivery and tracking. Unfortunately, mistakes do happen. My client's paperwork was never delivered and we didn't realize it for six months. What made it worse was that the client actually brought it to our attention by calling to inquire about the status of his case. The client was furious, to say the least. We had failed to catch this error.

I sought counsel about what to do—one person said to refund the whole case; another said not to refund but to call the client and outline steps to fix it. I took the second attorney's advice and called my client to explain the circumstances and to outline the steps we would take to resolve the problem. I let him vent. I let him say everything he needed to say.

I acknowledged his feelings. I apologized for the error. One week later, my client sent his brother and his parents to my law firm to start their cases; and his brother signed up on the spot.

Despite our problems, my client still trusted me and our relationship remained solid.

I hated delivering bad news to my clients, so I wouldn't close out cases that didn't have a favorable outcome because I felt so bad. I kept holding on, thinking that maybe I'd find some way to breathe life into a cold case. I'd tell the client, "I'm going to keep trying!" And in reality, I wanted to keep trying, even when there was nothing more to try at the time.

Even though I had the best intentions, I wasn't doing the client or myself any favors by dragging things out. I wasn't giving the client what he or she needed—closure.

I share this even though it is embarrassing because I want you to know that if you are struggling with this, you are not alone. As lawyers, it isn't easy to talk about mistakes. For me, not taking immediate action to communicate bad results with clients was a mistake that I kept making for years.

What You Need to KNOW:

- ☐ What your clients need from you
- ☐ How to make a first impression
- ☐ What might be causing your client's frustration

What You Need to DO:

- ☐ Improve communication with your clients
- ☐ Listen to what your clients have to say
- ☐ Avoid the pitfalls of over-explaining concepts in favor of keeping things simple
- ☐ Avoid miscommunication
- ☐ Deliver bad news to your clients clearly and concisely

Step 5

STREAMLINING YOUR LAW FIRM

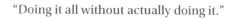

"Doing it all without actually doing it."

Streamlining and automation means freedom. If you streamline and automate your law practice, you will find freedom. You will not be chained to your work all day and night. You will work fewer hours and enjoy more time outside the office. You will finally free yourself of the feeling that you have to constantly be "on."

One of the questions that I am most frequently asked is, "How do you do it all?" I run a successful law firm. I host a weekly podcast called "6 Minute CEO." I run the Six-Figure Solo monthly membership. I write books. I started and continue to manage the Association of Mother Immigration Attorneys (AMIGA).

So, how do I "do it all"? My answer is simple: I don't.

I have found ways to streamline and automate my practice that are simply game changing. But this isn't how it always has been.

When my son was born, I found myself completely overwhelmed with trying to "do it all." I was handling a caseload, stepping into my role as the CEO of my law firm, managing home and firm finances—all with no staff and a 3-month-old.

I *could not* do it all. It's just not humanly possible.

But I was afraid to let go of the reins of anything. I didn't want to spend money on things that I thought I could "do myself." I was so scared that if I spent money on help, it would cripple me financially.

But as part of stepping into the role of CEO, I had to be realistic and mindful of my bottom line. My first book, *Be the CEO of Your Law Firm: Gain Control, Turn a Profit, and Reclaim Your Life*, discusses my journey from struggling day after day to managing a lucrative practice that allows me time with my family.

I learned how to take myself out of the middle of my law firm.

"Step 5: Streamlining Your Law Firm" is all about taking yourself out of the middle of your law firm. It shows you how to get the most out of your staff, your processes, and your clients by hiring based on your needs; avoiding the perils of over-hiring; maximizing and cross-training the staff you have; ridding your firm of the "wrong" clients; and decreasing your dependency on paper.

We will cover:

1. Hiring the Right Help at the Right Time;
2. Over-Hiring and Firing;
3. Streamlining Your Law Firm by Choosing the Clients That Are Right for You
4. Streamlining Your Law Firm to Increase Your Profits; and
5. Going Paper(less) in Your Law Firm.

Hiring the Right Help at the Right Time

Deciding to hire and hiring at the right time are two very important steps that every CEO of a law firm faces. Oftentimes, solos find themselves delaying the decision to hire and saying, "Well, if I can do it myself, why should I hire someone to do it for me?"

The problem is that doing it yourself limits you—your goal should always be to ensure the responsibilities you handle in your firm are things that only you can do.

Sure, you can complete forms, handle bookkeeping, run payroll, make copies, answer the phones, and more. But should you?

"Keep it small, keep it all." This means that when you do it all, you don't have to pay others. But it also means you won't get much work done either. Your firm will not grow and neither will your revenue.

For solos, it also means that more than likely, you are killing yourselves—and your businesses are suffering as a result!

Finding the right help takes time and patience. It also takes experience. Know that you might make a few mistakes along the way, but you will eventually find the right fit.

Start by redefining what "staff" means to you. It should no longer be "an in-office, 40-hour a week person." Being a business owner should force you to think differently in order to have your needs met.

Below are some examples of things you can try as you make your way toward hiring staff and outsourcing the right responsibilities in order to maximize the staff you have.

- *Phone Answering Service.* Use an answering service so the phones don't become overwhelming. The cost is much cheaper than having someone in the office, and the service helps schedule consultations and passes along client questions. *Ruby Receptionists* is a great option but there others out there.[1]

---

[1] Receive $75 off your first full month's invoice for virtual receptionist services when you mention AMIGA Lawyers or Ally Lozano.

- *Virtual Bookkeeping Service.* Unless you have the required training, a bookkeeper is incredibly necessary. The number-one task that lawyers say they are overwhelmed by is keeping track of the finances and doing taxes. Consider using *Bench*[2] for your bookkeeping. The monthly investment (which starts around $129 a month) will change *everything* for the better.

1. Take small steps forward

Letting go of the reins of your firm and your life can feel very scary; it requires a leap of faith. Actually, you don't have to take any leaps. You just need to take small steps forward.

You don't have to hire everyone at once. One small change can make a huge difference. Stretch your budget to cover one investment that will help you "do it all." Once you get comfortable with that, take on the next investment.

2. Determine which daily tasks can be delegated

This is the part that trips us up. We have every reason in the world for why every task we perform *should not* be delegated. One of the main excuses we give is, "I can do it better myself."

For at least one day, observe everything you do, such as: calling an insurance company about an insurance issue; researching a summer camp for your child; buying a birthday present for a friend; returning client phone calls; scanning documents; writing briefs; filing papers; planning a date night; and more.

For the purposes of this exercise, try not to make any judgments. Just look at each task neutrally to see if it can be delegated.

Hint: Everything I listed above can be delegated.

---

[2] Get 20 percent off for bookkeeping services from Bench for six months after a 30-day trial. Mention Amiga or Ally Lozano.

3. Delegate like a pro

One of the ways that we hold ourselves back from success is that we do not allow ourselves access to the resources we need in order to be successful. If we think we are under-earning and are barely making ends meet, we won't invest our hard-earned money in ways that would make our lives easier.

Unwilling or afraid to take risks will always keep us at a level below where we should be. Someone once said that Apple would never have been what it is today if Steve Jobs had refused to move out of the garage. Yes, he could have "kept it small and kept it all," but that is not the path to true success.

Success is not just financial, it is also personal. If you are trying to do it all, you are setting yourself up to fail either at home or at work, or both. You simply can't do it all.

Women lawyers, especially, find themselves trying to do it all and are pulled constantly between family and career—the brief writing, the laundry, the witness prep, the children's homework, the clients' questions, the doctors' appointments, the brief filing, and the family vacation planning.

One of the best ways to lessen this mental load is to delegate. You must delegate in order to have financial and personal success.

Of course, you probably have many excuses as to why *you* must be the only person to handle something. So ask yourself: "Am I really handling it or am I just barely handling it?" If answering honestly, you'd probably say, "Just barely."

That is because multi-tasking doesn't allow us to perform at our best; it only stretches us thin.

Delegating is a part of your role as the CEO of your law firm. Yet deep down, you probably think that no one can do the job, the task, the chore as well as you, the CEO, can.

Try this: Instead of comparing yourself to everyone by thinking, "Could someone else perform this task as well as I can?" try rephrasing the question this way: "Can someone else perform this task?" The answer should be, "Yes." Then ask: "Could having someone else perform this task allow me to focus on more important aspects of my business?" Again, the answer should be, "Yes."

Do not be afraid to delegate; it is the only way you will reach your true earning potential. By delegating tasks, you are not relinquishing your control, you are simply allowing someone else an opportunity to gain experience and improve his or her skills. You are not only helping yourself by delegating, you are helping the person to whom you delegate.

a. Contracting with professionals

One example of delegation in a law firm would be the use of contract attorneys for certain legal work. Using reputable contract attorneys can change your practice and your life significantly, whether you are a solo with no staff or a small firm with 20 people on payroll.

A contract attorney makes a living from writing briefs. He or she usually charges a flat fee, so there's no time to waste—he or she wants to get the job done.

Let's say you spend $1,000 on the brief, which might seem like an enormous amount when money is tight. But your money probably is tight because you don't have the time to devote to business development activities in order to bring in more revenue, or you're stretched so thin that you're struggling to earn retainers within a reasonable amount of time.

Paying a contract attorney $1,000 for brief writing could earn you $2,500 or more in retainer fees, or free you up to spend time on paid consultations that reap an additional $2,000.

These are just the potential financial benefits of contracting out work. There is also the mental benefit of not having to obsess over something that isn't getting done.

Using a contract attorney is one way to increase money in your law firm right away.

b. Using virtual help

Another way to take the pressure off yourself is to have a personal or virtual assistant to whom you can delegate those lifestyle tasks that take up brain space and energy—scheduling medical appointments for you and your family, planning a birthday party for one of your children, researching hotels for your next vacation, and more.

A virtual assistant can run $7–$15 per hour, well worth the peace of mind and stress relief.

Your goal should be to fill your workday with tasks that only you can do—tasks that are focused on making money. My workday is filled with consultations or client sign-ups—the things that bring in revenue for my firm—and I am the only one in my firm who can do them.

Other people can write briefs and legal arguments, prepare packets, complete forms, follow-up with clients, etc. Let those tasks be their focus while you make it rain.

Lesson Learned: A virtual assistant can change your life

When I first started out, I was a "true solo." I had no staff. The phone was going unanswered because I didn't like to answer it. My financial books weren't up to date because who has time for that when you are trying to be a lawyer and run a law firm?

My cases weren't streamlined—I was constantly chasing down clients for documents and then I'd get angry when they demanded that I respond to them right away.

There were cases I didn't feel like doing because I knew they were challenging or would take a lot of work and time, so I procrastinated. There were other cases that I wasn't doing because I just had to do "one small thing" and instead had more important things to do.

I refused to buy a faster office scanner because my scanner was "good enough," even though it was slow and I could barely get it to work. My only computer was crappy but it worked, so why would I buy a new one?

My baby was under a year old at the time and I was trying to be a stay-at-home mommy while handling my cases. I was barely earning any money, yet it felt like I was working 80 hours a week! I knew I needed help but didn't feel like I could afford the help. I felt completely stuck.

The only thing that could rectify this situation was to hire someone, but I had no money. I had one office that I leased in an office suite. Where would this person sit? What would this person do?

I reasoned that it would take me more time to get this person up to speed than it would for me to just do it myself. I finally decided to hire a virtual assistant and tried several variations—one virtual assistant at five hours a week, then three virtual assistants at five hours a week each. Finally, as luck would have it, I came across a virtual assistant who changed my life.

My virtual assistant has created contact lists, drafted business plans, and uploaded documents and client information to the case management system. She even started my e-file system and naming process.

I've had her design templates for many legal documents, including arguments. She taught herself how to handle much of the work we do. My husband and I own five companies and she is involved in all of them.

My virtual assistant now runs my life—medical appointments, relocation needs, shopping assistance, insurance issues, you name it.

After reaping the benefits of having a great virtual assistant on board, I decided I would hire someone in the office for five to 10 hours a week. Little did I know that she would end up going full-time after a week. The money, as disorganized as I was with it, figured itself out.

Business got better almost instantly. I started making more money than I had previously because I could get more done. I rented an additional office and never looked back. Now I have a team of six full-time staff in the office.

What excuses are you making not to hire? What do you fear?

You'll find that once you hire someone, your business will grow and expand and your only regret will be *not* having done it sooner.

My husband and I have a way of thinking that goes, "There's nothing that can't be undone." Let's say you hire someone and then you just can't afford to pay that person. You are barely staying afloat. You've cut every expense you can to make it work. You are ensuring you are maximizing that person's time.

Well, let that person go. That's the solution. Yes, it sucks to fire someone; but if you can't do it, you can't do it. It's not the end of the world. You can try again another time.

All of us have a breaking point. And we know that we can't keep up the pace. If you are asking yourself, "Should I hire?"—the time is now.

We must think of hiring as an investment instead of a cost. Staffing is an investment in your business, your life, and your sanity. It's an important investment at that!

Lesson Learned: Your business can grow if you let it

When I first realized I needed to bring in someone to help me with my business, I was really embarrassed to do so. I was completely disorganized and had no idea how to train someone. I felt ashamed of myself and my practice.

I was doing great work with great results, and my hard files were organized extremely well. I didn't miss deadlines but the firm itself was disorganized.

As a professional, an educated woman, a lawyer, and a business owner, I believed I should have had my business in a much better state.

Hiring someone involved getting over the shame that I felt—including the shame of my lack of money and lack of earnings.

I share this story because I want you to know that on the other side of your fear is relief. On the other side of your excuses and reasons why you shouldn't hire someone are all the reasons why you should.

When I was making excuses and feeling anxious about my disorganized business, I wasn't looking at the positive side of this change—that my business could actually grow if given the chance. I could rid myself of the constant fear and anxiety that something would be missed or that I wouldn't be able to get things done.

4. Decide whom to hire

Once you know it's time to hire, finding the right person can be tough. I recommend reading *Who*,[3] an excellent book that teaches you a lot about how to avoid hiring mistakes.

People say, "Hire slow, fire fast." Firing sucks, but it gets easier. It is important to let people go when it isn't working. You may do everything to find the right person and that person just doesn't work out. Let him or her go quickly.

Be prepared for staff turnover by always looking for your next hire. No matter how great your staff is, no one should be irreplaceable.

Think about it—people leave for all sorts of reasons (a spouse gets a transfer, someone has a baby, someone gets injured, someone burns out, or someone wants to return to school). These are all reasons out of your control—even if you are the best boss in the world and have the best benefits and are the greatest company, people leave. Being prepared means to constantly have your eyes and ears open for your next great team member.

a. Write a good job posting

This should not be your run-of-the-mill job listing. You need to think creatively about the kind of person you want to hire and who would make the right fit for you.

For example, if you don't like to micromanage but you want to count on people to get the job done, then you need a self-starter who is able to work without a lot of direction and be able to find information on his or her own.

If you are a perfectionist, you need someone who takes direction well, who does not mind working in conjunction with management,

---

[3] *Who: The A Method for Hiring*, Geoff Smart and Randy Street, with the following quoted content from the Greenhouse Blog. The book can be found on Amazon at *https://www.amazon.com/dp/1400158389.*

who is dedicated to working at the highest of his or her ability at all times and brings 100 percent to the table.

You know your work style and communication style best. You also know who would best complement you in the office.

Think about all the things you need done and make a list. Draft your job posting using your list. Then give the job a title. This will help you tailor the job description to meet the needs of your firm.

When I finally decided to hire legal staff, I interviewed an experienced, bilingual paralegal. She wanted more money than I could afford, but I believed that she would be the help I desperately needed and she would be able to work with very little direction.

Nevertheless, I knew that she was a few steps ahead of my needs at that time. She was at a place in her career where she was looking to come in, get the job done, and leave. But I really needed help getting organized and getting systems in place; I needed help building a business.

In the end, I decided to pass on that candidate even though she was excellent. She was not a good fit for my firm at that time. Eventually, I found the right person for what I needed.

b. Weed out candidates based on responses to the job posting

Attention to detail and the ability to follow basic instructions are important for any job, yet they are difficult skills to test in an interview. That is why the job posting should do more than merely explain the position and how to apply. Rather, it should list specific actions that you want the applicant to take, some obvious and some less obvious.

Try this: Include a note on the posting for the candidates to write a code word in the application materials to see if they can follow instructions.

You can say, "Be sure to include 'Immigration 2018' in the subject line along with your name." Then quickly weed out any job applications that don't have it.

Additionally, instead of just asking for a résumé, ask the applicant to include other application materials, such as a cover letter and reference list. If you are looking for a bilingual applicant, request a cover letter written in both languages.

This system helps weed out applicants quickly. Any applicant who does not follow the instructions you give should not be considered a candidate for the job.

Sample Job Posting

Law firm is seeking an administrative assistant. The position will be approximately 30–40 hours a week. Bilingual candidates only (Spanish/English). Please email application materials. Reference **Job KGL1117** in your application.

WHO YOU ARE:

1. You are a fluent Spanish speaker.

2. You are dedicated to excellent, top-of-the-line customer service.

3. You are organized.

4. You know how to use Microsoft Office and Adobe Acrobat.

5. You work quickly and efficiently while producing high quality work.

6. You are punctual.

7. You have an upbeat attitude and a desire to learn.

8. You care about the rights of undocumented Mexicans in the United States.

9. You can follow directions and work within operational systems by following a training manual.

WHO WE ARE:

1. Alexandra Lozano Immigration Law is a boutique immigration law firm located in Seattle (Tukwila), WA.

2. Our firm currently has a well-trained, efficient, and caring team composed of 1 attorney, 1 legal assistant, 1 admin, 1 virtual assistant (who is an LA as well), 1 law clerk, 1 business manager, and 1 assistant business manager.

3. We are a client-focused, results-oriented firm. Customer service and excellent results are our highest priority.

4. We take pride in changing people's lives despite the challenges posed in the current immigration system.

5. We work hard to keep our team limited to 40 hours a week because as much as we love our work, we also value our personal lives as well.

6. Our clients are the heartbeat of our law firm and we treat them with respect and dignity.

7. We have tightly-created systems that we value and continue to hone in order to improve, and we expect everyone to work within them.

8. We work together as a team in a way that is similar to an assembly line. No one person in the case handles any aspect of a legal case from beginning to end. We each have a well-defined role.

HOW TO APPLY:

Please email the following:

1. A cover letter detailing why you want to work for us and why you are ready to make this change in your career.

2. What you are looking for from a law firm environment.

3. Your resume.

4. 3 references who can be contacted immediately.

5. A few dates and times of when we can have a phone meeting.

Job Type: Full-time

---

c. Set up a phone screening interview

A phone screening interview saves you so much time. Instead of devoting 30–60 minutes of your day to an in-person interview, you can do a quick 15 minutes on the phone and go from there. This is something I have always done, and it's something recommended in *Who* as well.

Here are phone screening questions that are suggested from *Who*:

- What are your career goals?

- What are you really good at professionally?

- What are you not good at or not interested in doing professionally?

- Who were your last three bosses, and how will they each rate your performance on a 1–10 scale if we were to talk to them?

- What attracted you to this position?

- What makes you stand out from everyone else who has applied for this position?

My favorite question is: What are the things you do *not* want to do as part of a job? You will be amazed at the answers you get! Oftentimes, they will say they are not interested in doing one of the job tasks that you specifically need done. This is excellent information. It's something that probably wouldn't come up at any other time.

d. Email the candidate an activity to perform

If things go well over the phone, the next step is to send a short activity or task that you want the person to complete. It could be something that is performed regularly such as completing a form. You could develop a fake client and provide the candidate with some basic information to get the person started. See if he or she can complete the task to the best of his or her ability with the information provided, but be available to answer questions the candidate might have in order to complete the form.

This is a great test of resourcefulness. This will let you see whether a person can follow instructions as well as his or her attention to detail.

One time, I had someone complete a form and she made a spelling error in the name of the city. This was a problem for me because it showed that she lacked attention to detail, editing skills, and self-review, and that she couldn't do the bare minimum of copying and pasting.

You would think that candidates would try their hardest to impress you during the job interview and skills-testing process, so maybe this person doesn't work well under pressure. It helped me rule that person out quickly.

e. Arrange an in-office interview

There are various schools of thought on how to handle the in-office interview. The book, *The E Myth Attorney*, recommends doing an interview of all of your candidates together, that way you can see who excels and who falls off in a team setting. This could be a good idea if you have a large number of applicants/candidates. I have never had enough candidates to do this, though it does sound interesting. The book, *Who*, recommends a process that is more corporate-oriented, but there are great ideas that can be gleaned from it.

When interviewing, don't make the same mistakes I have made. I tend to make decisions based on "vibes," and I've also caught myself doing most of the talking instead of letting the candidate speak in response to my questions.

Here are some great interview questions, with some of them adapted from the book, *Who*:

- What were you hired to do?

- What accomplishments are you most proud of?

- What were some low points during that job?

- Who were the people you worked with? Specifically:

  a. What was your boss's name, and how do you spell that? What was it like working with him/her?

  b. What will he/she tell me are your biggest strengths and areas for improvement?

  c. How would you rate the team you inherited on an A, B, C scale?

  d. What changes did you make? Did you hire anybody? Fire anybody?

e. How would you rate the team upon your departure on an A, B, C scale?

- Why did you leave that job?
- What are your biggest accomplishments in this area during your career?
- What are your insights into your biggest mistakes and lessons learned in this area?

Additional questions:

- What are your career goals?
- What do you hope to accomplish in the next five years?
- If you could travel anywhere in the world, where would you go? Why?
- Who has been the biggest influence in your life? Why?

Here are some tasks that potential hires can perform:

- Use your training manual to do a task (*i.e.*, create a mailing label, set up a case in your case management system, etc.)
- Alphabetize something
- Do a sample declaration (*i.e.*, in our office, we have a template of questions that we use for declarations, so we have candidates ask us questions from the first page or two and then check their notes—it helps to see how fast they type, what they capture, see their writing skills, and more)
- Do a client interview using a template (with yourself acting as the client)

f. Contact references

Always call references! This is one of the biggest hiring mistakes I have made. I thought the candidate had performed exceptionally well during the interview process, so I hired without calling references. Every single time I have done this, the hire has gone disastrously wrong.

Here are some questions to ask when you call references (modified from *Who*):

- In what context did you work with the person?

- What were the person's biggest strengths?
- What were the person's biggest areas for improvement?
- How would you rate his/her overall performance in that job on a 1–10 scale? What about his or her performance caused you to give that rating?
- The candidate mentioned that he/she struggled with _____ in that job. Can you tell me more about that?

g. Make the offer

It's always great to make that phone call offering the job! Be sure to follow up with an email about the job specifics, including:

- Salary

- Start Date

- Schedule

- Office Attire

- Benefits Summary

The hiring process can feel stressful and overwhelming. Most of us wait until we desperately need someone before we make the decision to take on a new staff member. As a result, the hiring process can be rushed, making us settle for the wrong candidate or a "good enough" candidate.

Lesson Learned: Offer benefits for longevity

Recently, our insurance broker told us that the way to attract and keep great people is to offer benefits.

Health insurance may sound daunting, but it can be doable. An office-wide disability plan is cheap, about $35 a month, and is an easy benefit to set up.

There are a ton of different retirement plans to set up, and I know I have resisted because of the stock market; but as you grow and your tax liability severely increases, it will be something nice to have in place.

I recommend doing a simple IRA. You match the employees' contribution up to 3%, but if you pay someone $30,000 a year, that's only $900 for the entire year. Spread that out over 12 months, it's only $75 a month. It is a very small price to pay to help attract and keep great employees.

There are different plans that require the employer to contribute only if the employee contributes, but it's only up to 3–4%, which results in a small amount at the end of the day.

All of these things seem overwhelming, and they can be, but it is worth looking into these different products.

Over-Hiring and Firing

As lawyers grow, hire, and automate their law firms, they tend to over-hire. I get why this happens—once you start delegating and get the hang of it, it feels great. All of a sudden, you can breathe again. You can be a lawyer again, and that's why we started all of this to begin with! We became lawyers to practice law, not to run a business.

We begin to realize that we can do less while still running a profitable firm. So we delegate more and hire more. Then, we fall into the trap of over-hiring.

Once lawyers start over-hiring, their money and their profit margins are devoured by employee salaries!

Fellow solos and small firms have reached out to me in excitement because they've reached the seven-figure mark. Then, they tell me how many people they have on staff. I perform some fast calculations in my head and realize that these attorneys are barely making six figures because of the high overhead expense of salaries.

The key is to run your law firm as lean as possible. Utilize every single person and job in your firm for maximum productivity.

1. Don't sacrifice your firm to keep your staff

In the book, *Profit First*,[4] the author talks about how people will slash expenses and costs before they slash people. They find justifications to keep everyone when they could do the same amount of work with fewer staff. Or, they have staff whose roles could be better streamlined.

A consulting client of mine had two legal assistants who were not busy enough and one admin who was completely overburdened. This lawyer was also not growing in her business; she was stuck and couldn't go forward. She had streamlined herself completely out. In the past year, she had added three people to her team but her revenue hadn't increased. She was sacrificing her profits, which were quickly dwindling, with the intention of being more efficient. This is not the right balance.

In *Simple Numbers, Straight Talk, Big Profits! 4 Keys to Unlock Your Business Potential*,[5] the author discusses how people tend to over-hire when they start to earn more money, depleting all of the money from the firm—and not just the profit but also the firm's core capital target and tax reserves.

A perfect example of this is a previous employer of mine. This law firm always seemed to be on the verge of going broke. Paychecks for the partners would be suspended, yearly bonuses wouldn't be given, holiday parties would get canceled—all because the firm simply couldn't make ends meet. The firm was also months in arrears on its rent.

Lawyers are lawyers. Many are not good business people. They think that just because their numbers are growing and business is increasing that more staff is needed. But if your firm isn't operating efficiently—with no systems in place, no streamlined responsibilities, and no growth strategy—your firm is doomed to fail.

---

[4] *Profit First: Transform Your Business from a Cash-Eating Monster to a Money-Making Machine*, by Mike Michalowicz. Find it on Amazon at *https://www.amazon.com/dp/073521414X*.
[5] *Simple Numbers, Straight Talk, Big Profits! 4 Keys to Unlock Your Business Potential*, by Greg Crabtree, can be found on Amazon at *https://www.amazon.com/dp/1608320561*.

One of the reasons why my firm has been able to grow in staff while profits have continued to increase is because we do not rush to expand; we continually streamline roles to maximize what each person does, playing to their strengths instead of trying to overcome their weaknesses. Whenever things start to feel tight, we look at people's roles to see how they can be leveraged better, tightened up, and improved.

Right now, our team comprises six full-time employees, one part-time in-office contract attorney, and other contract attorneys used on a project-by-project basis. It allows us to keep a very high profit margin. I still focus on consultations and reviewing of work product, but I am "in" the business just enough.

I had experimented with taking myself out as much as possible, but things weren't going as well as they could have been. Being involved in my business in the ways that only I can allows me to maximize my time and my team.

Having experienced firsthand what can happen to a law firm that over-hires, I had developed a fear of hiring. But I have read many books on how to run a very lean business—maximizing staff, streamlining roles, etc.—so that I would never allow my hires to put me on a sinking ship—which leads to *everyone* drowning.

Lesson Learned: Don't be afraid to learn from other professionals

I am proud of my firm and what I have accomplished, but I also know that I need advice from other professionals to ensure that I am running my business in the best way possible and meeting the needs of my staff. So when I decided to bring in an external CFO—especially a CFO who has worked with some of the most prestigious law firms in the country—I was very nervous and almost resisted doing it. What if he tells me that everything I am doing is all wrong? What if he thinks I am stupid or inexperienced? And since I teach people how to run successful law firms, I feared that he might think it is ridiculous that I could teach anyone how to run a law firm if I am not running mine well.

Instead, he said that I was running the leanest, most well-run law firm he had ever seen. He told me what I was doing right and helped us use the data that we had been collecting to understand things like financial forecasting and setting up ways to "test" different scenarios—for example, what might happen if a certain case type slows down or if we were to make a high-level hire.

Because I overcame my fear of bringing in an expert, I have learned so much more about what it takes to run a successful business.

Do not be afraid to seek consultation from professionals who are outside of your expertise. Your law practice is a business and there are plenty of experienced professionals available to help take your business to the next level.

2. Perform financial forecasting

Performing a financial forecast can help show you the ebbs and flows of revenue within your law firm by tracking what months are your busiest or more lucrative. This data can help you decide whether and when to hire.

In order to determine the success of your law firm and what its future needs might be, you must track:

- Phone calls

- Consultations

- Contracts

- Every penny that comes into your law firm

a. Tracking phone calls

Give every person who answers phones a tally sheet with two columns—one for tracking each phone call requesting a consult, and the other for tracking phone calls that result in a contract. Every time they get a phone call for a consult, they will tally it under the contract column. And if that same person also signs up for a consult, it is tallied under the consult column.

It is important to tally in *both* columns if a person calls and signs up because you need to see your conversion rate.

Once you have this information, you can see how many calls you get each month; you can see whether different marketing efforts affect the numbers; you can even add to your tally sheet how people found out about you. You determine what your conversion rate is for calls to consults, and more.

This is very important information that will help you gain a full view of your firm.

We are just implementing it in my firm and I am really excited to get some good numbers and analytics from it.

b. Tracking consultations

Some people track consults and contracts throughout the year using a numbering system that covers the whole year, but this fails to give the data that you need in order to truly understand your business and make financial projections on a monthly basis.

It is more important to know how many consults you have on average per month; this allows you to see which months can be truly considered "slow" by looking at previous years' trends, and more.

Develop a consult tracking sheet by using Microsoft Excel or Google Sheets. Write the person's name, assign the person a consult number, and write how that person found out about you.

Use a numbering system that indicates what number each person is for the month. For example, my firm's number system would use C19-0207. The C is for consult, 19 represents the 19th consult for the month, and 0207 represents the date of the consult.

At the end of each month, the spreadsheet will show you how many consults you had and simply add the months to get a total for the year.

c. Tracking contracts

You need to have a separate contract-tracking sheet that uses similar numbering, but with no C in the front.

Write the client name, date of consult, date of sign up, how the client heard about you, the case type, and case amount.

I have not been adding the case amount to my spreadsheet and I regret it, so we are adding that in!

Your goal is to learn how many cases you are opening each month, observe any trends, and see how fast people convert. This also helps you see what your main case types are and how much you earn from each case type.

Build this into your case opening process to make it easier to record and track.

d. Use a backup system to track every penny in your law firm

No matter what programs you use for recording payments from clients, always have a backup system. This should be a spreadsheet that only you, and maybe your business manager, maintain and have access to. This system should include consults, monthly payments, new contracts, and anything else that brings revenue into your firm.

In my firm, my business manager logs every payment on the spreadsheet. He also checks the credit card processing every day to make sure that he has logged every credit card payment, and he checks our case management system to compare receipts to his list.

If you rely on just one thing, let's say QuickBooks or even your bank account, something will be overlooked—like the $100 that was paid in cash and wasn't deposited for some reason but needs to be recorded anyway. The spreadsheet serves as a backup record for human error—your assistant forgets to issue a receipt when she accepts a payment, for example, and then there is no record of the payment anywhere. Use a spreadsheet to account for every payment.

It sounds tedious but it takes about 30 seconds to log a payment into the spreadsheet. Tracking this information is really important for understanding whether you are meeting your goals and benchmarks.

A hiring decision should never be made without knowing where your firm's entire revenue is coming from and how it is being used.

Chapters 2 and 3 of my book, *Be the CEO of Your Law Firm: Gain Control, Turn a Profit, and Reclaim Your Life*,[6] walk you through exactly how to set up tracking for phone calls, consults, and contracts. They offer sample tracking sheets, forms, tables, and contracts to guarantee your success as you transition to your role as CEO of your law firm. These customizable documents are offered as a free download to book purchasers.

3. Establish tightly defined roles

Oftentimes, we over-hire when we do not have tight enough job roles and too many people are handling too many different roles. Your admin should be *just* your admin. He or she should not answer phones, file, process mail, and handle the firm's inbox while also being tasked with your firm's billing, human resources, and case preparation. This is inefficient. And you likely have other people who are doing all of these tasks as well.

Oftentimes, lawyers have their staff playing several roles within the law firm, such as having office managers preparing court filings and legal assistants performing collection calls. Then the lawyer thinks that everyone is maxed out, and the solution is to hire another person whom they then throw into this crazy mish-mash of responsibilities. Using your staff this way is completely ineffective and you are not getting the most bang for your buck.

Straighten out the jobs so each one is clean and streamlined. Make sure each person has a clearly defined job description and assigned duties so there is no overlap.

---

[6] *Be the CEO of Your Law Firm: Gain Control, Turn a Profit, and Reclaim Your Life* can be found on Amazon at *https://www.amazon.com/dp/1732082502.*

My firm clearly delineates the duties associated with each position. It is like the Henry Ford of law firms—similar to an assembly line where no one person is responsible for a case from beginning to end:

- I do the signup meeting.

- I complete the questionnaire with the client present (we developed a guide with the questions we always ask).

- The case goes to the virtual assistant and she uses my notes to draft documents.

- The virtual assistant then sends it to my in-office assistant.

- The in-office assistant prints the documents, prepares the case for my and the client's review.

- Everything is checked by me and then it goes to the client for signature while the client is still present or when the client is scheduled to return.

- The in-office assistant reviews the forms and the case in a meeting with the client.

This way, no one can de-prioritize a case or sit on a case. Everyone has very tight roles. The goal is to become systems dependent, not people dependent.

To make your firm run efficiently, everyone must have tightly defined roles and duties. Here are some specific examples from my firm:

Role: Legal Assistant

- Translate birth certificates
- Translate letters
- Translate marriage documents
- Open files
- Do client questionnaires for forms
- Collect client evidence
- Organize client evidence in e-files
- Organize client evidence in hard files

- Update evidence list with the client evidence
- Prepare filings for court
- Prepare filings for the government agency
- Mail FedEx filings
- Call clients to say that the filing has been mailed
- Update case status in MyCase from A/ P/ or Y
- Scan client docs
- Note what client docs have been received
- Process government requests for evidence
- Review forms with clients
- Review declarations with clients

Role: Virtual Assistant

- Prepare client forms
- Prepare client declarations
- Prepare responses to requests for evidence
- Prepare cover letters and legal arguments
- Submit case status inquiries with government agency
- Call agency hotline

Role: Administrative

- Close files
- Answer calls
- Return client calls
- Schedule appointments
- Put consults in MyCase
- Process mail
- Prepare and mail client FYI letters
- Prepare and mail monthly case status update letters to all clients
- Prepare and mail monthly case status update letters by specific case type
- Update case status in case information in MyCase
- Update case status in government agency database
- Calendar court dates
- Calendar government agency interviews
- File documents in hard file
- Scan mail

Role: Business Manager

- Conduct payroll
- Prepare and pay bills
- Manage bank accounts
- Process client payments
- Process receipts
- Manage client payment plans
- Manage firm benefits (such as health care, life insurance, disability insurance, etc.)
- Pay quarterly taxes
- Manage business license renewals
- Manage time off requests
- Hire and fire staff
- Ensure staff reviews are done
- Facilitate communication between attorney and staff
- Facilitate communication between attorney and clients
- Manage firm's marketing
- Manage business banking and contacts with the business banker
- Manage bookkeeping
- Manage communications with accountant
- Manage credit card processing

Role: Attorney

- Perform consultations
- Conduct sign-up meeting with clients
- Complete client questionnaires for forms
- Complete client questionnaires for declarations
- Prepare clients for court
- Prepare clients for agency interviews
- Review packets for submission
- Review legal work of the team
- Network, bring in new business

We also change as we add more team members and are always thinking of better ways to do things.

4. Establish a salary cap

Your payroll will be the highest expense in your business. It always will be. But that's where the concept of a salary cap comes in.

There is an actual formula you can use to figure out if you can afford to hire someone. I don't like sports analogies, but I have to make an exception in this case because this idea really resonated with me. The concept of a "salary cap" comes from sports, and here's how it works:

> In the NFL, every team has a salary cap—which is the total amount of money that the team can spend on hiring players. Let's say it's $100 million. This means that the total salaries for every position on the team must be equal to or less than $100 million. Each team can go for less expensive players in some positions and more expensive players in others. A team may need to decide whether to cut an exceptional yet expensive player in favor of replacing him with two really good players for the same amount. Every team must have a strategy—you can't spend $90 million on one great player and expect to fill a typical 53-man roster with the $10 million left over. The team must make smart money decisions.

Some law firms simply grow their staff as they grow their revenue without much thought about a salary cap or any sound strategy.

I have read more business books than anyone I know, yet the concept of a salary cap and an equation for calculating how much you can spend on staff is something I had never read before.

The book, *Simple Numbers*, describes an equation for reaching your own salary cap. It is more complicated than the equation offered by my CFO, but it is definitely worth the effort and is very important to know. Below, however, I am sharing my CFO's version of a salary cap equation, which is easier to summarize.

> No more than one-third, or 33 percent, of your revenue should be spent on salaries. This is a simple equation. If you go over that amount, you have exceeded your salary cap, which means your business could be headed for financial trouble.

I am committed to keeping my firm's salary cap at 25 percent or less, and it currently sits at 23 percent. My CFO says this is incredibly low, the lowest he has ever seen. And it includes my salary.

Let's say, for example, that you wish to hire an associate attorney and you are already at 33 percent—meaning you've maxed out your salary cap—then you must be sure that the hire will produce enough revenue to justify the hiring. If you are filling an admin position, then you should examine the rest of your team to ensure that everyone is producing at his or her highest level. Otherwise, you may need to make some staff cuts in order to bring on a new hire.

To determine whether your current team is maxing out at 100 percent, you cannot simply ask each person because the response will be undoubtedly, yes. Instead, look at your staff's output, turnaround times, and any other measures you have. How efficient are your employees? How many hours in an eight-hour day are they actually working at full capacity?

When calculating the true cost of hiring someone new, it is recommended that you add about 20 percent to cover employment costs. If you offer a $100,000 salary, the cost to your firm would be $120,000. This covers costs such as payroll taxes, benefits, vacation and personal leave, sick days, and more.

Though 20 percent is likely on the high side, when budgeting and determining payroll costs, it is better to be on the high side than on the low side.

When considering hiring, remember:

- Know whether your current employees are working at full capacity.

- Run every hire through the numbers before making a commitment.

- Calculate your salary cap and commit to keeping it at or below 33 percent.

The more you know about where your law firm stands, the more informed and strategic your decisions will be.

5. Make firing decisions swiftly

Firing sucks, but it is an inevitable part of running a business. Sometimes, people aren't the right fit. Sometimes, people are caught acting unethically. I have had to fire someone for lying and cheating before. I have fired someone because that person couldn't meet the job requirements. I have fired someone because that person couldn't keep pace. It sucked every time; no matter how right I was in making the decision. But every time, I think, "I wish I had done this sooner."

Oftentimes, we delay the inevitable, suffering the entire time. The longer you don't fire an employee who needs to go, the worse it will get. You will waste your time complaining and venting about the person, which eats up even more of the resources that are being wasted by having the wrong person on your team.

If you have someone on your team who is a gossip or who likes drama, *cut ties fast*. I know because I *was* that person (when I was an associate)—and it did a lot of damage. I should have been let go long before I actually was. Now that I have my own firm, I see how problematic this can be. A negative gossip will spread through your firm like cancer and will taint everything you have worked hard for.[7]

There are tons of excuses you can make for not firing someone. Remember, the next best thing is right on the other side of the decision that you are avoiding.

I heard something powerful at a conference once. Sometimes, someone in your business is an A player, but as you grow and your business grows, that person becomes a B or C player. It is important to recognize this and take swift action. As the saying goes, "What got you here won't get you there," and that goes for staff as well.

The lecturer said,

> "As I am saying this, if there is someone who pops into your mind, then it is time to let that person go. You know it and you can't deny it forever."

---

[7] I am embarrassed to share this, but I have learned from my mistakes and I want others to learn from them as well.

Your firm is your life line. Your clients are the heartbeat. If anyone is not bringing value to your firm and your clients, it is time for that person to go. If someone is causing you more stress than help, then he or she isn't the right fit. If someone has lied to you about little things over and over, then that person cannot be trusted with your business.

Safeguard yourself and your practice by having a lot of tools in place to make your expectations clear. Check in with your staff regularly.

Your law firm is about you first and foremost. You need a team that supports your vision and your dreams. You *deserve* that!

Lesson Learned: Don't use the office as your social outlet

Where we tend to go wrong as business owners is becoming too friendly with our staff. When I had my first legal assistant, I didn't really have any friends. I went to work and came home. I had a little baby and I was a new mom, so if I wasn't working, I just wanted to be at home with him.

When I was at work, I was getting social interaction. Short chitchat led to longer talks and then to longer conversations. Within a year, more than an hour a day had been wasted on sitting around talking instead of doing.

And then everything else started falling apart. Deadlines weren't being met. I felt bad to say anything because we were friends. She came in late—later than our "non-start" normal start time. I found her chatting on Facebook while in a meeting with clients. All sorts of things were going on that I didn't approve of and it was hard to put an end to it because we had become friends.

We usually have to make mistakes before we figure it out for ourselves. I had told myself that I would never let the friendship impact my business, but it happened.

I share this story as a cautionary tale.

Professional boundaries allow for you to be friendly with staff, but not turn your office into an all-day hangout.

Streamlining Your Law Firm by
Choosing the Clients That Are Right for You

The human element of lawyering means that sometimes we will encounter clients that are not right for us and our practices. Working with the wrong client makes everything more difficult; though you still provide excellent service and work quality, the case itself becomes draining. Working with the clients you really want to work with is another way to streamline your law practice.

The wrong clients tax resources. The story is the same every time: frustration, stress, and a constant feeling of "I'm not getting paid enough for this." Our jobs already require high levels of emotional resources to cope with the sad and difficult stories we hear on a regular basis, and the wrong client forces us to expel our emotions in ways that are unnecessary.

How do you manage the wrong clients? The secret is to figure out who the wrong client is before he or she ever steps foot in your office.

Ideally, we would notice in the consultation that the client simply isn't right for us, but that usually does not happen. Once we start the consultation, the human element comes into play. As an advocate deeply committed to the cause, an unlikeable client with a compelling case makes it hard to say "no." Other times, financial pressure or concerns cause us to take a case we wouldn't otherwise accept.

This is why it is important to have a plan before the consultation starts. You need to take a hard look at your current caseload and determine if there are any "pain spots," meaning clients or case types that drain you and/or your firm of resources.

Let me explain.

While reviewing my caseload and planning for the new year, I realized there was a small fraction of clients who qualified for a certain type of case but those cases were causing me the greatest amount of stress. Almost every client in this small fraction of cases was difficult.

These were the clients who were constantly questioning my work and whether I was doing the job properly. They were also disproportionately less forthcoming with evidence and more difficult to get the right documents from in order to make a strong case. Every step felt like a battle.

When I looked at my cases neutrally, I could see that this certain type of client comprised less than 5 percent of my business yet caused about 90 percent of my stress. The extreme disproportion made me realize that it wasn't worth continuing to take on those cases anymore.

I called a team meeting to discuss it. Every member of the firm agreed that our resources were being drained by this particular type of client. Now we have processes in place to screen for those wrong cases.

Here are a few questions to ask yourself to help identify what types of clients and cases are wrong for you and your practice:

- Is there a type of case that stresses you out more than any other case?

- What is it about the case type that you don't like? Is it the legal issue? The type of client involved? The way that the opposing party handles that type of case?

- What percentage of your caseload involves case types you don't like?

- What type of case typically attracts difficult clients? What percentage of your caseload involves those cases?

Getting honest about your caseload allows you to provide the best service and experience to the right clients for you and your firm.

You may be thinking, "But if I say no to cases, what if I don't have any business?" This would be the perfect time for you to concentrate on defining who your ideal client is.

My book, *Be the CEO of Your Law Firm: Gain Control, Turn a Profit, and Reclaim Your Life*,[8] is the culmination of all my efforts toward building a profitable and sustainable law practice. Chapter 1, "Creating Your Vision and Strategy," offers practical tips and exercises to help you define your ideal client and build your ideal law firm.

Knowing who your ideal client is and how to target him or her will allow you to increase your personal satisfaction with your cases and your firm. You can fall in love with your practice again.

Streamlining Your Law Firm to Increase Your Profits

What happens as we grow as solo practitioners is that we become the center of the firm. The firm literally depends on us; you may have one great assistant who knows a lot, but without you, the firm would implode.

What this means is that you are like the sun in the solar system—everything revolves around you. You have to keep everything together. You have to keep everything flowing. You are constantly interrupted because you are the only one who knows the answers—whether it is a client question or a procedure question or a supplies question—only you know everything.

This means that the firm is operating off your memory and your self-systems. This will make you implode mentally and physically, and it is unsustainable.

Streamlining your law firm is *the* way to make your law firm more profitable. Law firms often are not valuable as businesses because the lawyer is tied to the value of the law firm. This means that we are

---

[8] Find *Be the CEO of Your Law Firm: Gain Control, Turn a Profit, and Reclaim Your Life* on Amazon at *https://www.amazon.com/dp/1732082502.*

dedicated to case work and case management instead of master-minding work flow and cash flow.

Our law firms should run like Starbucks. Starbucks is successful because it has policies and procedures in place so that every Starbucks is run exactly the same regardless of the location.

Think about it: From the way that Starbucks takes your order to the way it processes your order to the way that it makes your drink, everything is always done the same way—whether you are in Japan, Mexico, or in the original Starbucks in Seattle. Your law firm needs to run this way.

As the CEO of your law firm, it is up to you to develop procedures so that your law firm can run like a well-oiled machine. It is important for anyone to start working at your firm and be able to get to work right away by following the policies and procedures that you have in place.

Once you have people on board, you can start streamlining your law firm. It takes planning and organization, but you will have more time to handle those functions once you have people to help you out.

I made it my goal to have my law firm fully streamlined. The streamlining has made an incredible difference to my bottom line. My employees are happier and feel more satisfied because they understand the expectations of their positions and their roles more clearly.

By streamlining the law firm, our entire team has shifted from being reactionary (*i.e.*, trying to remember where the template contract was saved to be able to put the case together, etc.), to being proactive and deliberate about each action in our law firm.

Here are some ways to help you get started on streamlining your firm:

1. Use a case management system

If you don't use a case management system, start immediately. Whether you have five cases, 50, or 500, you must start now. I use MyCase, but I do have partnerships with Practice Panther and Clio.

Whatever system you decide to use, make sure *every* case is entered in the case management system. Make sure every contact with your firm is logged in. Stop emailing within your firm about cases. All messaging needs to be within the case management system and linked to the case.

A case management system puts you on the path to overseeing your firm without actually being there. You can see every call, every contact. Your staff can reach you about a case without flooding your email.

2. Create a training manual

The training manual is key to onboarding any new employees and helping to ensure that everyone in the law firm can do any job at any time if needed.

Here is the quickest way to create a training manual:

- Ask every person in your firm to bullet-point every single thing that he or she does in a day. Put a deadline on it, such as "in 1 week from today I need you to send me your bullet point list."

- Ask each person to write step-by-step how to do each thing on the list. By doing this, you will quickly make progress on your training manual.

Some essentials for a law firm training manual are:

- Steps for processing mail[9]

- Scripts for answering the phone[10]

---

[9] See a sample from my firm's training manual below in the section on Going Paper(less) in Your Law Firm.

- How to open a new case

- How to close a case

- Steps for processing hearing notices

- How to calendar deadlines and important dates

The objective of the training manual is to ensure that any person can join your firm and get started right away. It also allows everyone in the office to assume any part of a case and be able to take the next steps.

In addition, as the boss, you should know how to perform the job of every person in the office, or at least have a way to figure it out, in case you are ever short an employee due to unforeseen circumstances. Even if you have no staff, you should create a training manual. Like any good business, your firm will eventually grow and this document will become necessary. You will be glad that you put in the effort beforehand.

3. Create a process for naming and organizing e-files

As more firms turn toward digital files and paperless offices, it is becoming increasingly important to find a way to keep e-files just as organized as physical files. Creating template e-files by case type is very helpful.

In the template e-file, you can pre-name all the folders and internal documents that you need in order to complete a particular case type.

Templates serve almost no purpose if they are difficult to find or disorganized. It is important to have a streamlined way to manage your pending cases.

---

[10] In chapter 4 of my book, *Be the CEO of Your Law Firm: Gain Control, Turn a Profit, and Reclaim Your Life*, I offer sample scripts for phone contact, consultation confirmations, and in-person greetings, which you can put to use in your law practice right away.

My firm uses Dropbox for Business as our server. All documents are saved there.

Here is a screenshot of the main screen of our firm's Dropbox:

This is how my firm handles e-filing:

Many of us rely on scanning documents into our e-files, but they are not truly organized. It is important to find a way to organize all of your e-files so that you are consistent and can find documents whenever you need them.

The idea of creating a uniform way to name every scanned document was revolutionary to me. It has made everything so much more organized and easy to find.

This certainly can be a time-consuming task, but it is worth the effort. This is something for which you can enlist the help of a virtual assistant or intern.

The entire firm is organized around one folder—the *"File Setup Folder."* It is the Master folder.

The File Setup Folder is organized by case type; within every file setup folder are the templates that correspond to the case type. It sounds confusing, but continue reading because it really isn't difficult at all.

Here is a screenshot of the different file setups we have.

Inside every file setup are internal files. Every single e-file has these same internal files.

Every single template is in the corresponding e-file.

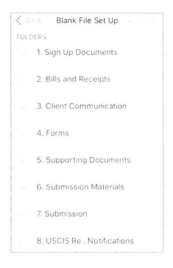

For example, in the I-360 file, here is the "1. *Sign Up* folder":

At sign up, we do the contract, the fee waiver, the I-360 with AOS questionnaire, and the I-360 Declaration Guidance Questionnaire. They are all in the sign up folder.

Within the "3. *Client Communication Folder*," we have every single FYI letter we have created listed by case type.

The documents are numbered in order of what will happen in the case—Copy of Submission, Receipt Notices, Biometrics Notice, Work Authorization Approval—this way, it is easy to see what has been done. We also have them separated by language, both English and Spanish. We do not use any forms software because our system is faster than the forms software.

What we have in our "4. *Forms Folder*" is every form related to the case type; this way, our virtual assistant can quickly complete the forms based on the client questionnaires.

The "5. *Supporting Documents Folder*" is where the legal assistant scans in all of the client's documents and saves them according to our naming key. (*e.g.*, "Birth Certificate-USC Daughter- Leslie- CRUZ, Juan").

Create a Name Key where you list every document with the way you want the name formatted. For example: "I-130 Receipt-LAST NAME, First Name," or "Engagement Letter-Case Type-LAST NAME, First Name."

In the "6. *Submission Materials Folder*," we keep every template that is necessary to prepare the legal case. This includes the case summary sheet, case cover letter, legal argument, and the index of documents.

The "7. *Submission Folder*" is where we scan a copy of the full submission.

The "8. *USCIS Receipts and Communications Folder*" is where we scan in each receipt notice and other agency communication.

Each document is scanned separately and named according to our naming key (which always includes the client's name).

Our e-file organization has decreased the time we spend searching for templates and other often-used documents. Also, it allows us to easily find exactly what we need in each client's e-file. It has been a complete game changer.

Once a client signs up, copy the folder and paste it into the *"Open Cases Folder."*

The files are organized by case type and then client name, making everything easy to find and easy to organize. Everything is ready to go in the file; all you need to do is customize the templates for each client and case.

4. Provide a quote sheet and document list during the consultation

Though most attorneys provide a quote sheet with the case type at the consultation, something that many of us do not provide is a list of the required documentation that you will need to start the case.[11]

I was afraid to do this at first because I feared that I would be encouraging clients to do the cases themselves. I can tell you now that this was completely unwarranted. In fact, it had the opposite effect. The clients come in fully prepared at the time of sign-up and it saved us months of having to chase after them for documents. This has allowed our turn-around time on certain cases to be much faster.

5. Create templates for client communication

No matter how well an attorney can explain the steps in a case, it is difficult for a non-lawyer client to understand what it is that we do. Client communication letters provide overviews of the entire case process and what steps will be taken in the case.

---

[11] I discuss in more detail the use of handouts, quote sheets, and document lists in the section on Incorporating a Sales Presentation into Your Consultation Without Sounding Salesy under Step 3, "Conquering Sales with Confidence and Authenticity."

Each time you submit something in a case on behalf of your client, a client should receive a letter explaining what was submitted, what is coming next, and the overall case plan.

Though you may want to tailor letters to each specific client, it is still important to have templates that can be used and modified throughout a case. This saves time, cuts down on phone calls, and clears up unnecessary confusion.

6. Start the case immediately at sign-up

Having a quick turnaround on a case usually requires a client's cooperation on many levels. Before streamlining, it would sometimes take months to start a client's case because the client would not respond to us with the information or documents requested.

My firm schedules up to three hours for sign-up during which we go over the contract, obtain the necessary information we need to complete any forms and questionnaires, and start on the declaration (depending on the case).[12]

We provide clients a list of what we need before they even sign up; by doing so, we can start work on their case the moment they sign the contract.

If you bill hourly, this method can help you earn most of the initial retainer right away, which increases your monthly earnings.

> Below are examples of checklists and work flowcharts to help guide your staff and streamline and automate regular processes in your law firm. Some of the content is immigration-law specific, but the concept can work with any law practice.

---

[12] Step 4, "It's All About the Client" provides additional guidance on starting the contract-signing appointment. See the section on Nurturing Plus Over-communication: The Building Blocks of a Solid Attorney/Client Relationship.

Case Preparation Flow Chart

Case Step Number	Case Step	Team Member
1	Consultation	Lawyer
2	Sign up appointment to start the case	Lawyer and/or Legal Assistant
3	Open the physical and e-files	Admin Assistant
4	Prepare forms, declaration, and legal argument	Virtual Assistant
5	Prepare submission packet and do initial review of everything prepared by the Virtual Assistant	Legal Assistant
6	Initial review of packet	Lawyer
7	Meeting with client to review forms	Legal Assistant
8	Final review of packet	Lawyer
9	Scan and submit packet	Legal Assistant and/or Admin Assistant
10	Email client copy of packet with FYI email	Customer Service and/ Admin Assistant
11	Monthly email update letters	Customer Service

Sign-Up Appointment Checklist

- Go into ALIL server → ALIL file setup, then choose the case type that the client is signing up for. Copy (don't cut) the file and paste it under ALIL Server → Clients → Open Cases → [case type]
- Prepare contract
- Print out 2 copies of contract
- Review contract with client
- Have client sign the contract
- Give the client his/her copy of the contract (in a branded folder if he does not have one with him)
- Take payment from client
- Email Manuel to tell him about the payment
- Prepare receipt/Manuel prepares receipt (depending on whether he is in-office)
- Change the MyCase letter from Z- to A-
- Change the MyCase case type from consultation to the type of case that you are opening
- Collect documents from client in support of his case
- Open folder 1. Sign Up Documents
- Open the form questionnaire PDF
- Use the client documents to fill in as much as possible and ask the client anything that you can't easily ascertain from his/ her documents
- Save the questionnaire as you go
- Once you complete that questionnaire, have the Administrative Assistant come and make copies/ scans of all of the documents that the client brought in
- If there is a declaration that needs to be done, use the declaration guide questionnaire and go through all of the questions for it
- Save the questionnaire as you go
- Once you finish, schedule the client a time and date to come back in 1 week to sign forms and declaration
- Send the Virtual Assistant a MyCase message to tell her that the case is ready to prepare (and assign a Legal Assistant, if applicable)

Preparation of the Submission Packet

☐ Get the hard file of the case

☐ Go into submission materials and print out the case cover letter

☐ Assemble the documents in the hard and e-files according to how they are listed in the case cover letter

☐ Review the forms against the documents to make sure that the information in the forms is correct

☐ Print out the legal argument and review for typos/errors

☐ Use post-it notes to note any questions about the forms, documents, or legal argument for the lawyer

☐ Indicate with small sticky notes where the lawyer needs to sign

☐ Rubber band the packet to the top of the file and give to the attorney for review

Initial Review of Packet

- Pull up the consultation notes in the MyCase system
- Review the forms and legal argument to make sure all of the information there is consistent with what was first stated in the consultation (*i.e.*, if there was an expedited removal that was mentioned in the consultation, information must be included in the packet)
- Review the legal argument for accuracy as well as typos
- Review the forms for accuracy as well as typos
- Review questions from the Legal Assistant and respond via sticky note
- Make changes as needed by hand and put a sticky note to indicate where you made changes
- Rubber band the packet to the top of the file and return to the LA to make the edits

Meeting with Clients to Review Forms

- Bring the entire packet to the meeting and turn just to the forms pages
- Go through every single line of every single form with the client, ensuring that everything is 100% correct. Confirm every date and every name/spelling.
- Have the clients sign and date each form after they have confirmed everything is correct.
- If there are changes that need to be made, instead of making them on the spot, you can make them by hand and mark them with sticky notes to be able to complete the changes when the clients leave.
- If you had to translate the forms, be sure to sign them and date them.
- Fill in the date on the attorney's signature line before giving to the attorney.
- After the client leaves, make the final changes.
- Put a sticky note where the attorney needs to sign.
- Provide the file to the attorney for a final review.

Final Review of Packet

- ☐ Go through the forms and legal arguments one last time
- ☐ Sign all the forms
- ☐ If there are any final changes, then note them with sticky notes
- ☐ If the packet is final with no changes needed, put a sticky note on top that says "ready"
- ☐ Give the file back to the Legal Assistant

Going Paper(less) in Your Law Firm

Today's definition of a paperless office is one that has significantly reduced or eliminated the use of paper and has made it much easier to do work from a remote location.

Many law firms are converting to a paperless office to be more money conscious, environmentally friendly, and more mobile.

But no law office can go totally paperless. I'm sure that day will come, but for now, let's focus on using *less* paper by calling it paper(less).

If your law firm is considering going paper(less), there are a few things you should consider before you make the leap.

1. Keep a hard file

Every case should have a hard file for things, such as the original client documents and the original contract. Most documents need to be stored somewhere until they are ready to be used for a legal filing. Sometimes, there are documents for which an original signature is needed but the document itself may not be mailed or used right away (*i.e.*, signed release documents).

Oftentimes, there are papers that need to be printed and saved in the hard file for the attorney's case preparation. For example, for all court cases, I copy every submission that I make to the court and keep a hard file that matches the court's file.

A hard file for each case can be a backup measure to ensure that every case is properly entered in the electronic system and has a corresponding e-file and hard file.

Once a month, go through your case list and match hard files to e-files to ensure that every case is properly entered into all electronic systems (such as case management system, QuickBooks, and accounting programs, etc.). It also gives you the opportunity to close out completed cases.

2. Invest in a good scanner

For example, do not copy, print, or retain any unnecessary paperwork. Find ways to recycle paper (*e.g.*, make them into notebooks or use them for court notes).

I had a 3-in-1 office printer/scanner/fax, which worked okay but not great. My scan function was very slow and it often jammed or did not save properly.

Then I found the ScanSnap, and it changed everything. The ScanSnap scans extremely fast and with great accuracy. We also have an Epson scanner that works nearly as well.

Standalone scanners are an easy way to ensure that everything in the office is scanned and saved properly. It is worth the investment.

3. Create a concrete way to process mail and client documents

By creating systems and processes for how to handle incoming documents, they will ensure that you stick to the paper(less) practices you have created. It is helpful to have a Microsoft Word or Google Docs document, which outlines how to process mail and client documents.

Below is an example from my office training manual. This has helped ensure that we have a consistent process for scanning documents into the server:

Processing Mail

- First, scan all of the mail together into one document.
- It will automatically save to the desktop.
- Once it is saved on the desktop, call it: Mail Scan- Date (YY-MMDD) (*i.e.*, Mail Scan- 16-0321)
- Cut it from the desktop and save it to "Mail Scans" file on the server
- Email the scan to attorney
- Then scan each document individually. Rename the PDF to reflect the name of the document and then the case

> name (*i.e.*, Biometrics- I-918- RODRIGUEZ, Juan; see below for naming guide)

Cut the document from the desktop and save it into the client's e-file.

Make a note in MyCase stating what the document is.

In the title write "received _____ in the mail."

In the body write, "This has been scanned and saved into the client's e-file."

If it is a decision, a notice, etc., prepare an FYI letter

- Server → Templates → FYI Letters
- Choose the FYI letter that applies to the case
- Prepare the FYI letter tailored to the client
- Print the letter and bring the letter plus the notice to the lawyer to review and sign
- All documents should be submitted to the lawyer with the hard file. Rubber-band the documents to the outside of the file and place in the lawyer's inbox.
- Scan the signed letter with the notice and save into the client's e-file
- Send the letter

Make a note in MyCase about what was mailed

If it is a receipt notice, log on to USCIS.gov and add it to Case Status Online account

- https://egov.uscis.gov/casestatus/displayLogon.do
- Username:
- Password

Once you log in, you can add the case right away with the receipt number. The tracking number is the client's full name.

For many years, I have run a mostly paper(less) office. Recently, I made some tweaks that make "going paperless" work even better and more efficiently for my firm.

Many attorneys are making the switch to a paper(less) office. You likely have some sort of paper(less) practices in place in your firm right now.

What You Need to KNOW:

☐ How to hire the right help at the right time

☐ What type of help do you need for your firm right now

☐ What types of clients and cases cause the most stress and can you do without them

☐ If you have staff, are they being used to their full capacity

☐ What percentage of revenue is committed to salaries

What You Need to DO:

☐ Remove yourself from the middle of your law firm

☐ Hire based on your needs

☐ Avoid the perils of over-hiring

☐ Perform a financial forecast

☐ Maximize and cross-train the staff you have

☐ Establish tightly defined roles among your team

☐ Establish a salary cap

☐ Rid your firm of the "wrong" clients

☐ Decrease your dependency on paper

ACHIEVING SUCCESS IN WORK AND LIFE
Accepting Accountability & Responsibility

"You have to take charge of every situation and hold yourself accountable."

Do you tend to start projects but are rarely able to finish them? Does it seem as though you're always falling behind in your tasks? Are you constantly rushing to meet deadlines and feeling overwhelmed, constantly moving but never getting anywhere?

If you answer, yes, to any of these, there is no doubt you are exhausted. There is no doubt that you are under-earning. There is no doubt that you need to hold yourself fully accountable, accept it, make changes, and take steps toward getting yourself some help.

Accountability is what is missing for so many of us. We have so many things that we want to do, need to do, and "should" do. But we don't do them or we need to be reminded to do them. We refuse to hold ourselves accountable for our actions or inaction.

The only person who can change things is you. You can have every excuse in the world why things aren't going well for you right now—you don't have time to put into the business, you don't have time for everything you need to do, you don't have money to invest in the things you want or need.

I get it.

Sometimes things are hard. Sometimes they are really hard. Occasionally, they are unbearable.

Taking responsibility requires a paradigm shift, one that requires us to release the victim mentality and move forward.

No one is going to be knocking down your door, desperate to give you an opportunity, just like clients aren't going to beg you to come and find them so they can hire you. You have to take charge of every situation and hold yourself accountable.

Lets' say you're having a slow month. Instead of saying, "It's January, it's just slow" (which makes it sound as though the situation is out of your control), take control immediately. Ask yourself, what action can I take to bring in more business?

- Try calling previous consultations to follow up and see if you can get them in the office for another face-to-face meeting.

- Record a 90-second video about your area of practice and post it on social media.

- Go on Facebook and do a live video.

These are quick things that you can do. But note that they require effort. You have to put forth the effort. You cannot hope that someone will push you to do it. You cannot wait for someone to do it for you.

You have to take action and hold yourself accountable for results.

Accepting accountability can be difficult because it can elicit shame and self-judgment. We may feel embarrassed about what we haven't accomplished. We might try to blame others or our external situations for why we have fallen short. But we must hold ourselves accountable despite this.

Do not rely on family members or anyone else to help hold you accountable—you either have to be fully accountable to yourself or you need to hire someone who will help hold you accountable.

"Step 6: Achieving Success in Work and Life: Accepting Accountability & Responsibility" focuses on building accountability and efficiency in your personal and professional lives. You'll find ways to minimize activities performed in your firm that waste time, as well as tips to reduce distractions in order to increase your efficiency.

We will cover:

1. Identifying Seven Wastes in Your Law Firm;
2. Finding Ways to Work Smarter Not Harder; and
3. Calming the Social Beast.

Identifying Seven Wastes in Your Law Firm

Waste: to use or expend carelessly, extravagantly, or to no purpose.

In the 1990s, Toyota Manufacturing implemented a practice of identifying seven wastes to increase revenue.[1] Though the concept was originally created with factory production in mind, it can be adapted easily to law firms.

Increase your law firm's efficiency by identifying, reducing, and even eliminating wastes. Increasing efficiency will help you maximize your time at work and give you more time for life.

---

[1] *The Machine That Changed the World*, published in 1990, outlined Toyota's lean production system and was based on a five-year study conducted by MIT.

The same thought process can be applied to your home life; by streamlining certain processes (chores, anyone?), you can reduce waste and spend more time on the really fun stuff!

Waste #1: Transportation

> *Movement of work between areas that does not add value.*

This refers to the act of moving someone or something from one place to another.

- Are you taking time to mail bills when you could e-bill?

- If you do detention or criminal work, can you designate a certain day each week that you'll visit the detention center or penal institution rather than going every time you get a call?

Waste #2: Inventory

> *More materials/information on hand than is required.*

Simply put, it means having too much stuff. Take a good look at your office (and your home, too).

- Are there old files to scan and destroy?

- Do you have unnecessary clutter? Are there unused items (old books, office supplies, etc.) to donate?

- Could you transition to a paper(less) office?

- Could you downsize to a smaller but more efficient office space? Or open a virtual law office?

Waste #3: Motion

> *Unnecessary movement of yourself and your staff.*

While transportation is the movement of work, motion is the movement of actual people.

- Are files kept in an easy-to-access, central location?

- Are you traveling to a meeting/appointment in person that could be handled via Skype or Zoom?

- Are you moving from your desk to the printer to retrieve printed documents that could've been emailed instead?

Waste #4: Waiting

Any delay between one process ending and the next step beginning.

Waiting for the processing of cases or information from clients is a time waster.

- Evaluate the process you use to request paperwork and proofs from clients; can anything be improved?

- Is the document list you give to your clients clear and concise?

Waste #5: Over-processing

Adding more value to a service or product than customers want or will pay for.

This is a big one for lawyers. Over-processing is creating more work for you than is necessary.

- When doing work-related tasks from home, is it necessary that you do it right then or can it wait until you're back in the office?

- Is it crucial that you answer that email during family dinner or can it wait?

- Are you doing more work for the client than necessary?

- Is the client paying you to complete the work to that level of detail?

Waste #6: Over-production

When more time and resources are used on a project than is necessary.

- Are you spending more time formatting documents and making them "look good" than ensuring that the legal and documentary requirements are satisfied?

- Can you streamline an elaborate client tracking system by using a simpler case management system?

Waste #7: Defects/Rework

    Errors or mistakes causing the effort to be redone.

- Have you streamlined your workflow to include self-checks and self-review to avoid small mistakes?

- Are your processes documented or do you have a training manual with instructions on how to do everything in your office—from processing the mail to preparing certain forms?

- Are you asking the clients the right questions upfront?

I challenge you to develop ways to become more efficient by increasing your firm's use of technology or finding better ways to use the current technology you have in order to cut down on time-wasters.

Finding Ways to Work Smarter Not Harder

Our profession wears over-working as a badge of honor. How many times have you heard attorneys "complain" about the amount of hours they work? Complaining is our way of bragging. We brag about our billable hours. We've all done it.

But shouldn't we be focusing on ways to work smarter not harder?

For years, I would go to bed but couldn't sleep; my mind would be racing with things that needed to be done. I was constantly in panic mode and on the verge of an anxiety attack. I couldn't rest. I always felt there was something more to do, something I had forgotten, or something that I was on the verge of forgetting.

Some lawyers I know sleep with notebooks beside their beds because they awaken in the middle of the night with thoughts about a case and will write them down to ensure that they don't forget. Their minds are always working.

But overworking leads to under-earning. If you are always on, always working, and always connected, you cannot be earning what you deserve. There is no amount of money that is worth sacrificing your sanity. Yet, that is what so many of us are doing.

It's time to change. You know your family needs you. You know you want to be more present in their lives. You are working non-stop, can't sleep, can't rest, can't ever get anything done.

The solution? Get more done.

Doesn't that sound crazy? But it's true. Getting more done means becoming more efficient in the use of your time. Getting more done in less time is the way to increase your profits, improve your life, serve your clients better, and show up better for your family.

If you want to serve your clients in the best way, you need to have resources so that you aren't overwhelmed and suffering from burn-out.

Efficiency helps us work smarter and get more done. Efficiency requires targeted, laser-focused effort and your full attention. The following list consists of actions you need to take to become more efficient in your life and your law firm:

1. Create systems that bring balance to your life;
2. Use every minute of your workday wisely;
3. Decline difficult clients; and
4. Restrict personal phone use at work.

These things will help you get more done while maximizing your life and your profits, because when we talk about earning more money, we are really talking about having a better life.

Lesson Learned: You have the power to change

For years, I was earning $20,000–$30,000 a year, struggling to make ends meet, constantly overdrawing my account, and always fearing that the money would run out. I didn't charge my clients more because I cared. I didn't focus on billing because I felt money-hungry and it felt somehow wrong. I thought that if I truly cared about my clients and the cause, then I couldn't and wouldn't focus on money. So things were bad ... and then I lost everything in a hurricane when I was seven months pregnant.

At that moment, I knew I had to change. I could wallow in my situation, or I could make things better. I didn't have money. I didn't have a place to live. I didn't have any of those things. But every one of those things was something I had the power to change.

1. Create systems that bring balance to your life

For some people, mornings are chaotic, but that's usually because there is no system or routine they follow each morning. Even though a routine can get boring, a well thought-out system will *always* work.

Systems make you more efficient *and* they use up less of your brain power. The author of *Your Brain at Work*[2] reinforces the idea that systems minimize distractions and use less brain energy. As a result, we are able to make more money and enjoy life more.

Not only can your personal life benefit from systems, but a fully systematized law firm can make your professional life easier. Your firm should run like a Starbucks. No matter where you go in the world, your experience at Starbucks is the same. This is no accident. Everything is highly systematized; this way, nothing gets missed.

---

[2] *Your Brain at Work: Strategies for Overcoming Distraction, Regaining Focus, and Working Smarter All Day Long*, by David Work, can be found on Amazon at *https://www.amazon.com/dp/0061771295*.

You need to have systems for the way phones are answered, clients are greeted, cases are opened and closed, sign-ups are done, and more.

I find routines boring. I get stir crazy if I am at home too long or not actively doing something with my time. But as a business owner, mother, and wife, I believe in the benefits of having workable systems in place to maintain order on a regular basis.

Life is too busy to leave it all to chance. That being said, you need systems in every area of your life. Systems allow for self-care. They help honor your time and preserve your brain power.

Once you have systems in place, you will find it easier to ward off distractions. Distractions will not fit in your system; systems will allow you to stay on course and finish whatever you started.

Implementing systems for your everyday tasks and your law firm will transform your practice and your life.

2. Use every minute of your workday wisely

Even with tight systems in place for structuring your day, you can still fall prey to distractions. Starting each day with a set of goals and a modest to-do list can help maintain some structure and keep you on track to accomplish what you set out to do.

a. Start modest with daily goal setting

A long list of goals or things you need to accomplish in a day will only serve to create angst and frustration when you fail to accomplish everything. So let's start by being realistic. Having 20 items on your list isn't realistic and will only have the opposite effect of making you feel like a failure.

Start with three primary tasks, nothing more. And at the end of the day, whether you've accomplished all three items or not, celebrate what you were able to do. Remember, even small accomplishments matter.

For example, a daily goal of mine is to review at least one finalized file, which I can do in about 10 minutes. Between consultations, I might have about 5 minutes, but I start anyway because my next appointment might run 5 minutes late. Or if I run 5 minutes late for my next consultation, I know that my staff will make sure that the person is well cared for and comfortable while he or she waits.

Instead of spending 5 to 10 minutes scrolling through my Facebook posts, I choose to maximize that time by accomplishing something that seems small but is quite significant; it's one less file on my desk and one more case being moved to the next step.

b. Focus on your business

During your next break, take action. Maybe you've been meaning to look for some marketing tips for your business but you haven't had the time. If you have 15 minutes between client meetings, listen to a marketing book on Audible. Or listen to a lawyer marketing podcast to gain some helpful tips. Most podcasts run 15 to 30 minutes and can fit into your day between consultations.[3]

Let's say that you need more business, so you commit to calling a past consult during every break. Whether you are leaving messages or speaking directly to the person, you'll see the benefits of your follow-up quickly when money starts flowing in.

Structuring your day with specific goals will help you maximize your time and your profits. Once you decide to maximize every single moment of your "free time," and hold yourself fully accountable, you are going to be amazed at how much you can accomplish. You will be able to work a 40-hour workweek again. Or less. I guarantee it.

Lesson Learned: Make life's little moments more meaningful

I took a look at my phone screen usage and found it to be extraordinarily high. I blamed it on not really having anything else to do when I'm at home with my kids

---

[3] I publish the "6 Minute CEO" podcast that's short enough to fit into any schedule and is packed with powerful tips that you can implement right away. Visit *http://www.allylozano.com/podcast/*.

because I don't really enjoy playing kids' games or watching kids' movies. I felt I was being productive when I was only being about 5% productive and 95% unproductive—and all I was doing was feeding into my social media addiction.

I realized I wasn't enjoying all that scrolling anyway. So I cut my social media engagement to only three times a day—once in the morning while exercising, another time around noon, and in the evening after the kids go to bed.

Now while I'm with my kids, I read a book or listen to an audiobook while they have fun. Or I will work on a project that I can do while lounging in my son's bed as he plays while still able to interact with him.

3. Decline difficult clients

Most attorneys can tell which clients will be difficult right from the beginning. It is best to decline those cases from the get-go. The amount of time and energy will be disproportionate to the amount of money you will earn from working on the case.

It is a good idea to determine whether you are taking on the wrong clients for the practice you would like to have.[4] Get help developing your ideal client with tips and exercises outlined in chapter 1 of my book, *Be the CEO of Your Law Firm: Gain Control, Turn a Profit, and Reclaim Your Life.*[5]

4. Restrict personal phone use at work

In order to move quickly through a task, you need to stay focused and move the distractions out of the way. Consider implementing a "no personal phone" policy in your office. Throughout the day, those beeps and pop-up notifications are very distracting. Even one pop-up on the screen can break your concentration.

---

[4] For more on how to stop servicing the wrong client, read the section on Streamlining Your Law Firm by Choosing the Clients That Are Right for You under Step 5, "Streamlining Your Law Firm."

[5] Find the book on Amazon at *https://www.amazon.com/dp/1732082502.*

In my firm, our policy requires that personal phones be off or silenced. We even have a drawer designated for phones. Everyone gets to pull his or her phone out once every two hours for five minutes.

Since I have a 4-year-old, I don't want my phone to be completely off, so I keep the ringer on but place it in the drawer. I have found that having the ringer on makes me check my phone less often than having it on vibrate because there's no need to "double check" to make sure nothing was missed.

Making small but significant changes in your daily routine can make a world of difference. These tips are designed to help you release some of that tension and anxiety and get your mind back on track.

Calming the Social Beast

The internet, social media, and email drive our personal and professional lives. With all the advances that cyber connection has brought, it also has the consequence of never letting us turn off.

If you're anything like me, you're relentlessly bombarded with emails, texts, social media alerts, phone calls, and voicemail—all of which are vying for your attention. As a result, you're probably forgetting to respond to important messages while other messages are simply getting buried beneath the digital heap.

If this sounds anything like you, then a "Cyber Cleanup" is in order.

1. Delete the social media app

Which social media apps drain your time and energy the most? For me, it's Facebook. Delete the app. Without the app, you will not receive automatic notifications, which means you will *not* be compelled to check your social media constantly. By forcing yourself to log in to a social media website through your browser, you will be more mindful each time you pull up the page. It gives you a moment to ask yourself, "Do I really need to check this right now?"

Once I deleted the Facebook app from my phone, I became more mindful of the amount of time I spent scrolling through my phone every time I received an alert. I now only check my page once a day, and it is freeing.

Some people advocate for deleting Facebook permanently, but Facebook is an important business tool. I have my firm's page, the page for the Association of Mother Immigration Attorneys, and other professional Facebook groups I belong to because they are all good for business development.

If Facebook is part of your business marketing strategy, you must remain engaged but do it in a way that won't mindlessly monopolize your time.

2. Be ruthless with your inbox

We reason with ourselves that we are going to revisit certain emails, or that we are "saving" an email for later. Due to the sheer volume of emails sitting in our inboxes, it is nearly impossible to go back through and peruse the "important" emails we save.

If you have thousands of emails in your inbox, it's time to get ruthless. Imagine using the "cyber" version of a machete to chop away at your inbox. It's called the delete button. Delete, delete, and then delete some more. If there are emails that are truly special or important, create a folder for them and move them out of the inbox.

Seeing that number go down is extremely gratifying and freeing. It is akin to decluttering your house, and it also helps declutter your mind.

Once you put these steps into action, you are on your way to making your cyber life more manageable.

3. Unsubscribe/rollup email lists

Unroll.me = Game Changer.

This website, *Unroll.me*, helps clean out your inbox. It searches your inbox to see what email lists to which you are subscribed and will unsubscribe you. For example, it will find emails from Alaska Air deals, Expedia communications, and inspirational emails from people you follow (like Kris Carr, Oprah, etc.).

It identifies each email and asks you if you want to either "Keep it In Your Inbox, Unsubscribe, or Add it to the Rollup." The Rollup is a once daily email that has every email subscription in it.

This process is done in about 10 clicks or less. Using Unroll.me helps limit the constant email checking because you will receive fewer emails.

Another great part of Unroll.me is that it constantly monitors the inbox for subscriptions to add to the Rollup and makes unsubscribing easy.

What You Need to KNOW:

☐ The activities that waste the most time in your firm

☐ What causes chaos or panic in your firm

☐ How much time you spend on social media

☐ What social media apps you can do without

What You Need to DO:

☐ Minimize activities in your firm that waste time

☐ Create systems for your personal and professional lives

☐ Delegate tasks you don't need to do

☐ Decline difficult clients

☐ Disconnect from the overwhelm of social media

☐ Set achievable goals every day

CONCLUSION

"Thrive: to grow vigorously, to flourish."

The *Merriam Webster Dictionary* defines the verb, "thrive," as the ability to gain wealth and prosper; to grow vigorously, to flourish.

Six-Figure Solo: Transform Your Practice from Surviving to Thriving is all about raising your law firm to a prosperous and wealthy level. This book is meant for those who want their law firms to flourish and grow vigorously.

You've decided that you no longer wish to survive from one day to the next. You want your business and your life to thrive. But in order to attain this level of success, you must be willing to put aside your fear, take risks, and seek help, support, and advice from those who have reached their goals but continue to raise the bar higher for themselves.

If this sounds like you, then you've come to the right place. Is it possible that you might not agree with everything I've written in this book? Yes. But I challenge you to maintain an open mind and try some of the suggestions outlined in this book before you judge one way or the other.

I offer this advice because when I first started and was looking for help, I couldn't find much at all. I had to cobble together bits and pieces from different books that were mostly outdated in order to figure out for myself what was useful and what wasn't, what seemed to be working and what didn't work at all.

Is this book the panacea for your law practice, the secret to success? It could be. My methods have helped many solos and small firms go from floundering to flourishing. It's up to you to take what I provide to you and tailor it to fit your specific needs.

This book is chock full of great tips to help grow your business. But if you don't gain anything else from it, I want you to walk away with the following valuable lessons from each chapter:

1. Determine your profit margin and pay yourself a salary

Step 1: Getting Paid

If you find yourself thinking, "Why would I focus on profit margin when I have a ton of work to do?" then know that this is your limiting belief and an old story that does not serve you well. You are a CEO and a lawyer. They are separate and distinct roles. They are different and must be treated differently.

Many of us are not paying ourselves. We are settling for what is leftover at the end of each month instead of being more strategic. Paying yourself a fair market value salary is one of the most important tasks you will perform as a business owner—and you deserve it.

2. Branding your firm: Are you Walmart or Neiman Marcus?

Step 2: Taking Your Law Firm's Brand to the Next Level

Don't be an accidental Walmart. Is it your business plan to have the lowest prices on the market? If so, there is absolutely nothing wrong with this. However, deciding to be the low-cost leader must be purposeful. Many solos and small firms end up with prices that are low because they don't feel empowered to charge more or they feel bad about increasing their fees.

Understanding what your clients want will help you determine price and also determine how to interact with your clients in a way that is meaningful for them.

3. Incorporate value-based quoting into your consultations

Step 3: Conquering Sales with Confidence and Authenticity

Selling is all about leading with the *value* of your services. This is such a significant statement and one you must remember as you start to think about how you can focus on the value of what you provide to your clients.

It's all in how you communicate. People do not walk away from a contract because of price. They walk away from a contract because they do not understand the value they will receive from signing a contract with you. Value comes from knowing the wants and needs of your clients.

4. Handle client misunderstandings with empathy

Step 4: It's All About the Client

"I understand." These two words are so simple and yet so powerful when spoken to calm or diffuse a heated situation. What the client really wants from you is to be heard and understood, not brushed off or interrupted. Hear the client out. Be sincere in your response. Make concrete plans to avoid misunderstandings in the future.

5. Establish a salary cap

Step 5: Streamlining Your Law Firm

There is a formula you can use to discover whether you can afford to hire someone. Remember:

> **No more than one-third, or 33 percent, of your revenue should be spent on salaries. This is a simple equation. If you go over that amount, you have exceeded your salary cap, which means your business could be headed for financial trouble.**

Your numbers matter—a lot. By focusing on revenue in your law firm, it does not make you less of a lawyer. Protect your business at all times, do not over-extend yourself, and do not sacrifice your profits for staff.

6. Find ways to work smarter not harder

Step 6: Achieving Success in Work and Life

Efficiency is what allows you to work smarter and get more done by delegating work, establishing systems and routines, eliminating distractions, and choosing your clientele more strategically.

These things will help you get more done while maximizing your life and your profits. You really can earn a great living and do great work. They are not mutually exclusive.

My Final Note

Six-Figure Solo: Transform Your Practice from Surviving to Thriving is written from the heart and the desire to see others experience the success that I have. Don't hesitate to let me know how you're doing. Contact me at *ally@amigalawyers.com* and share your experiences.

Please feel free to offer a review of the book through Amazon; or e-mail any words of encouragement and constructive criticism to the publisher directly at *tatiatroy@ramseshp.com*.

RESOURCES

1) Practice Advice

- *Six-Figure Solo Membership: Ally Lozano provides strategies on how to grow your law firm*
  - http://www.allylozano.com/shop/#ShopSolo

2) Ethics Opinion

- *Does your client need fee financing? New ABA ethics opinion provides guidance:* ABA Journal *Online, Nov. 27, 2018*
  - http://bit.ly/ABAnews

- *ABA Formal Opinion 484*
  - http://bit.ly/ABAOp484

3) Books

- *Who: The A Method for Hiring,* by Geoff Smart and Randy Street
  - https://www.amazon.com/dp/1400158389

- *Profit First: Transform Your Business from a Cash-Eating Monster to a Money-Making Machine*, by Mike Michalowicz
  - https://www.amazon.com/dp/073521414X
- *Simple Numbers, Straight Talk, Big Profits!: 4 Keys to Unlock Your Business Potential*, by Greg Crabtree
  - https://www.amazon.com/dp/1608320561
- *Your Brain at Work: Strategies for Overcoming Distraction, Regaining Focus, and Working Smarter All Day Long*, by David Work
  - https://www.amazon.com/dp/0061771295
- *Be the CEO of Your Law Firm: Gain Control, Turn a Profit, and Reclaim Your Life*, by Alexandra Lozano
  - https://www.amazon.com/dp/1732082502
- *Law Firm Business School: The MBA for Your Law Practice*, by Alexandra Lozano
  - https://www.amazon.com/dp/1732082529
- *The E-Myth Attorney: Why Most Legal Practices Don't Work and What to Do About It*, by Michael E. Gerber, Robert Armstrong & Sanford M. Fisch
  - http://bit.ly/amigaemyth
- *Work Happy: What Great Bosses Know*, by Jill Geisler
  - http://bit.ly/amigabosses

4) Podcasts

- *Gen Why Lawyer: "Implementing great systems and building a 7-figure practice with Ally Lozano"*
  - http://www.genylawyer.com/158-2/
- *The 6 Minute CEO Podcast: Making small changes one billable increment at a time*

o   http://www.allylozano.com/podcast/

5) Client Payment Options

- *iQualify Lending: a lending company that offers loans to cover lawyer fees.*

  o   https://www.iqualifylending.com/allylozano/

6) Cloud-based Legal Practice Management, Case Management, and Customer Relationship Manager Software

- *Practice Panther: Get 10% off your first year*

  o   http://mbsy.co/practicepanther/33906256

- *Clio: Provides custom demos for your firm. Works directly with your firm to get your data into the system*

  o   http://app.clio.com/signup/?referral_code=AP-AMIGA

- *MyCase*

  o   www.mycase.com/

- *Less Annoying CRM*

  o   www.lessannoyingcrm.com/

7) Administrative Outsourcing

- *Bench: Get 20% off for bookkeeping services for 6 months after a 30-day trial. Mention Amiga or Ally Lozano.*

  o   https://bench.co/partner/6-minute-ceo

- *Ruby Receptionists: Receive $75 off your first full month's invoice for virtual receptionist services.*

  o   https://www.callruby.com/amigalawyers/

- *Gusto: Get a $100 gift card to Amazon for signing up for payroll, benefits and HR services.*

  o   https://gusto.com/r/0MIdD/?utm_source=reflink

- *Uber Conference: Web and phone conferencing*
  - www.uberconference.com/

8) Design Services

- *Conception Logo: design services*
  - https://conception-logo.com/en/

- *Vistaprint: affordable customized products*
  - www.vistaprint.com

9) E-mail Campaign Service Providers

- *Mailchimp*
  - https://mailchimp.com/

- *Aweber*
  - www.aweber.com/

- *Constant Contact*
  - www.constantcontact.com/index.jsp

- *Vertical Response*
  - www.verticalresponse.com/

10) Online Marketing Websites

- *Avvo*
  - www.avvo.com

- *FindLaw*
  - www.findlaw.com

- *Google My Business*
  - www.google.com/business/

- *Yelp*

- o   www.yelp.com

- *Yellow Pages*
  - o   www.yp.com

11) Social Media Platforms

- *Facebook*
  - o   www.facebook.com

- *LinkedIn*
  - o   www.linkedin.com

- *LinkedIn's Playbook*
  - o   http://bit.ly/LIPplaybook

- *Instagram*
  - o   www.instagram.com

- *SnapChat*
  - o   www.snapchat.com

12) Video Hosting Websites

- *YouTube*
  - o   www.youtube.com

- *Vimeo*
  - o   https://vimeo.com/

- *Periscope*
  - o   www.periscope.tv

- *BeLive.tv*
  - o   https://belive.tv/

13) AMIGA Lawyers Facebook Videos

- *Are Excuses Holding You Back from Success?*
  - http://bit.ly/amigavid1

- *These Four Numbers are Crucial to Your Law Firm's Success!*
  - http://bit.ly/amigavid3

- *The Four Things You Need to Stop Doing in Your Law Firm Today!*
  - http://bit.ly/amigavid4

14) Miscellaneous

- *My Fonts: See a variety of fonts and how they are used*
  - www.myfonts.com

- *Unroll.me: This website searches your inbox to see what email lists to which you are subscribed and will unsubscribe you.*
  - https://unroll.me/

INDEX

Y

Z

ABOUT THE AUTHOR

In 2012, after becoming disillusioned with the practice of law in traditional firms, Alexandra Lozano decided to start her own firm to escape what she described as "toxic, cutthroat, and unsupportive work environments."

But her launch into solo practice almost didn't happen. Alexandra's experience working in traditional firms had such a profound impact on her that she almost quit practicing altogether. After leaving her last firm, she relocated to Mexico to recuperate and rejuvenate while deciding whether law practice was really in her future. Alexandra's husband implored her to remain engaged with the law, convincing her to start her law practice and manage it from Mexico. She agreed. There, Alexandra spent the next two years running her Seattle law firm from Cabo. She made it work by convincing herself that she "only needed a law firm earning in pesos" to get by.

Then disaster struck. While visiting Seattle to attend her own baby shower, Alexandra and her husband lost everything they owned in Cabo to a hurricane. Pregnant and practically penniless with only the belongings she had brought with her for what should've been a short trip, Alexandra and her husband were stranded in Seattle, one of the most expensive cities in which to live in America.

Faced with rebuilding her life while maintaining her law practice, she pushed on; and with the birth of her son, everything changed. Alexandra realized that she didn't become a lawyer to be poor and needed more out of life than the feeling of doing great work for her clients. Within three months of giving birth, Alexandra had rehabilitated her practice and was now heading a profitable legal business making six figures. Her three-month transformation from earning pesos to earning six figures is a true example of her determination, fortitude, and zest for life—three characteristics that she uses to fight for her immigrant clients every day.

Alexandra is a nationally recognized, award-winning immigration attorney. She is the founder of Alexandra Lozano Immigration Law PLLC, based in Seattle. In addition, as the founder and CEO of the Association of Mother Immigration Attorneys (AMIGA), Alexandra teaches other attorneys how they can transform a simple law practice into a thriving business.

Through AMIGA, Alexandra empowers other attorneys to be the CEOs of their law firms with a weekly blog and webinars, Six-Figure Solo membership, inspirational 6-Minute CEO podcast, regularly scheduled Ask Ally coaching conference calls, and the annual Women, Power & Money in-person conference where she provides women attorneys with step-by-step guidance on how to perform the work they love while also running a profitable legal business.

In 2016, Alexandra received the American Immigration Lawyers Association Sam Williamson Mentor Award for "outstanding efforts and excellent counsel to immigration attorneys by providing mentoring assistance." Her alma mater, the Seattle University School of Law, also bestowed upon her the distinguished alumna award for "her tireless advocacy on behalf of undocumented immigrants and her innovation in creating a national network to support immigration attorneys who are women and mothers."

Alexandra and her husband share five children and are happily living in the Seattle suburbs.

Become a Six-Figure Solo!!!

Visit http://www.allylozano.com

TIER 1: EXECUTIVE

The Executive level is ideal for new solo practitioners or associates currently aspiring to start their own firm. Value-priced but full of invaluable social networking access and monthly educational programs.

TIER 2: SOLOPRENEUR

You're already out there on your own, working hard to make big things happen. With added VIP access to my Business Vault, and my Business Bootcamp course, I can help you push past any barriers to bring those big plans to fruition.

TIER 3: CEO

With direct access to me in my Private CEO Facebook group, plus access to the Women, Power & Money live event, this is my hands-on package for helping you bring about the greatest improvements to your law practice in the shortest time possible.

ALLY LOZANO SALES ACADEMY

Stop under-earning today! Learn Value-Based Quoting and start earning your worth. In just 6 weeks, you and your firm will be transformed with Ally Lozano Sales Academy.

EXECUTIVE-TO-EXECUTIVE CONSULTING

Key takeaways from our time together:

1. Gain more clients and charge what you really deserve

2. More time and freedom to build a life that supports you
3. Learn how to effectively streamline your procedures

Register at
http://www.allylozano.com/shop/

Made in the USA
Coppell, TX
22 January 2020